ST79200 H8-1
087-403-4604
to 4.95
S0-DMY-613

OLD TESTAMENT

You Are There

In Bible Times

By Bev Gundersen

illustrated by Lorraine Arthur

Library of Congress Catalog Card Number 88-90717
ISBN 0-87403-460-4
Copyright ©1988, Bev Gundersen
Published by The STANDARD PUBLISHING Company, Cincinnati, Ohio.
A division of STANDEX INTERNATIONAL Corporation. Printed in the U.S.A.
13-02356

Contents

To the Teacher:

Have you ever wished you had a new way to present Bible stories to your class—some new way that would involve your students and show them a realistic portrayal of Bible people and truths, applying all of it to contemporary times?

Then enter into the living world of the Bible as this book, *You Are There,* does just that—allows each student to become a part of the story as an eyewitness. YOU are allowed to actively enter into the customs, culture, and everyday feelings that the people in that period of history knew. As the student becomes the character called YOU, as a slave to a harsh master, a child in a family, or an exile in a strange land, he or she will experience the emotions and thought patterns of people who saw God at work in their times and situations.

The lessons have been prepared with an attempt to incorporate activities that can be done by one child as well as a class of several children. This is to enable them to be used by the home school program as well as by Christian schools and Sunday schools.

YOU

Each story has an eyewitness called YOU. These characters are identified at the beginning of each story. The student is to pretend he or she is this person called YOU. This gives the feeling of being *there* when the story actually happened. Of course, the stories are fictionalized to permit this YOU ARE THERE view.

Accuracy

Life in Bible times is portrayed as accurately as possible through research into the manners and cultures represented in each story. These have been woven throughout the stories in conversations and actions. The detailed facts of the period will be etched indelibly in your pupils' minds. By finishing the stories as first-person reports, the children will realize that the relevant truths in the story will come alive. The endings can be completed either by using them as creative writing projects or group discussion periods.

Fascinating Facts

Fascinating Facts are given for each story to provide background information on the customs and culture of Bible times. They make the stories more interesting and meaningful as well as easier to understand.

Each fact has been thoroughly researched for accuracy by the author.

"God's word is alive and working ... And God's word judges the thoughts and feelings in our hearts."—Hebrews 4:12

Share and Compare

These Share and Compare sections at the end of each chapter give a review of facts and principles in the stories. They can also be done as written assignments or class discussions. By referring to Scripture portions

surrounding and related to each particular story, the students will get the whole picture, not just an isolated passage removed from its Bible context. Questions concerning sequence of events, classification of Biblical or pretend people and events, and match ups of people and descriptions are mixed with those that make the pupil apply the answers personally.

Activities

Each chapter also has two activities. The aim of one of these is to reinforce a particular Christian trait the story has illustrated. Such characteristics as trust, forgiveness, and obedience are treated in these activities. They make use of such methods as finger puppets, games, and participation activities to bring these traits out in life applications.

The second activity in each chapter is to teach a memory verse which coincides with the trait taught in the Bible story. These activities use mazes, codes, and puzzles to reinforce the Scripture passage and make memorization easier. The International Children's Bible has been used for all Scripture references for this book. This version is written on a third grade reading level and is the easiest for young children to understand.

To God be the glory!
Bev Gundersen

To
Tom and Carol
who recognized the gift
and
my church family of Salem Covenant
whose prayers made it possible

Mission Impossible

GENESIS 24:15-67

> YOU are Keren-Happuch. (CARE-un-HA-puck)
>
> She is the maidservant and friend of twelve-year-old Rebekah.

YOU hurry to catch up with Rebekah who always seems to be at least one step ahead of YOU. Although YOU are her servant, you are also best friends. This evening you have been talking together about a very important matter.

"Rebekah, are your father and brother really looking for a husband for you?"

"Yes, Keren. YOU know that I was twelve at the Feast of the New Moon. Laban says that he is the only one in all of the city of Haran with a marriageable sister who has no promise of betrothal."

"But surely your father would not arrange a marriage for you with someone who worships the moon god? Bethuel has always said that he serves Jehovah only."

Rebekah stops still and smooths back a curl of shiny black hair. She turns and frowns at YOU. "Keren-happuch! Do YOU think that Jehovah cannot take care of those who love and serve Him? He knows all that we need. We can trust Him to provide everything that is necessary for us."

"Even a husband who loves the Lord?" YOU ask.

"Even a husband!"

Rebekah smiles and you continue walking together down the hard-packed, dirt path.

YOU glance sideways at YOUR mistress. She is very pretty and YOU know that if it were not for the requirement of worship that her family has set, she would have any number of choices for a husband. And then, what would become of YOU? YOU have been her servant and best friend since you were both little. YOU cannot imagine life without her around.

YOUR thoughts are interrupted by a glad little cry from Rebekah. "Look, Keren, there is a caravan at the well! Perhaps we can hear news from as far away as Nineveh or Carchemish. Hurry."

The leader of the caravan, an older man, is standing with his head bowed. Some men servants are making the ten camels of the caravan kneel down. YOU see that this is no ordinary group of traders. Their camels have only a few packs, but YOU note that several have large baskets strapped to them. YOU wonder about the purpose of the baskets.

YOU and Rebekah hurry past the men and camels to fill your jars from the well. Just as Rebekah returns to the path, the older man runs to her.

"Young maiden, may I have a drink from your jar?"

Rebekah quickly lowers her jar and holds it out for him. Even before he is finished drinking, she offers, "I will water your camels too."

YOU watch, wide-eyed, as Rebekah rushes back and forth from the well and pours water into the leather trough from which the camels drink. It seems like an endless task, for the thirsty animals eagerly drink great amounts of water.

The leader reaches into a small bag and gives a gold ring and two golden arm bracelets to Rebekah. "Who is your father?" he asks, "Would he have room for us to stay in his home tonight?"

Before you know it, you find yourself back at home, and Rebekah is eagerly telling her family all about the stranger and his gifts.

"You left him at the well?" Laban asks and dashes out the door. Before long he is back with the men and animals.

"Don't just stand there, Keren," Laban says, "The guests are almost done washing their feet. We must have the food ready immediately."

But when YOU offer the men food, they refuse it. Their leader announces, "I will not eat until I tell you why I came."

Late that night YOU stare wide-eyed at Rebekah. "I can hardly believe it," YOU say.

"He asked the Lord to help him find a wife suitable for the son of his master Abraham by sending someone to water his camels? Who has ever heard of choosing a bride in such a way? Why, he was still praying when we came along. Can the Lord answer our prayers before we are done praying? And then to find that the woman he chooses is a member of his master's family. The whole thing is impossible!"

Rebekah's flushed face is triumphant. "Not impossible, Keren. Didn't I tell YOU the Lord would provide everything that is necessary for us? Even a husband who loves and serves Him as we do?"

"But to think that your family agrees you are to marry this Isaac. They know nothing about him. Because his mother is dead, you would have to run the household all by yourself. You might never even see your family again. What would become of you—of me?"

"Oh Keren! YOU are what is impossible! Don't YOU see that this is clearly from the Lord? Will YOU never learn to trust our God to guide and help us? Jehovah will take care of YOU, of me, of both of us."

YOU are not convinced. "Well, I for one am glad that you will have some time to think it over. Now, let's look at the gold and silver jewelry and robes he gave you."

Early the next morning at breakfast, YOU nearly drop the tray YOU are holding when YOU hear what Abraham's servant says.

"It is time for us to go. Let me take Rebekah and return to my master."

Despite the protests of her mother and brother, the servant insists on leaving. With YOUR heart pounding against YOUR ribs, YOU rush outside where YOU meet Rebekah just returning from the well.

"Rebekah! They want you to go with them— NOW! They say you are to decide what you want to do. What will you do?"

"Do? Why I will go with them, of course. Jehovah has planned this for me. I trust Him to know what is best."

In an unbelieveably short time, YOU are packed and standing beside Rebekah, waiting to be helped into one of the large baskets hanging on each side of the camels.

"Isn't it good that Father has given me YOU, Julia, Anna, and my old nurse Deborah, as bridal gifts?" says Rebekah, as she hugs you. "We will go to Beer-Sheba together. I told YOU the Lord would care for us."

As the caravan moves away from Haran, YOU take one last look at YOUR home. What will YOU find at the other end of this long trip into the unknown? YOU blink back the tears and pray for protection. THEN ...

Read Genesis 24:62-67 and write/tell the awe-filled ending to this story as **You Are There.**

Fascinating Facts

There are two kinds of camels. Some have one hump while others have two. The camels in Israel were the ones with one hump. A camel's hump weighs about eighty pounds. It stores fatty matter which provides energy for the camel. When the animal has gone for a long time without food or water, the hump almost disappears.

Both of the legs on one side of a camel move forward at the same time, which gives it the strange rolling gait that can cause seasickness for those riding these "ships of the desert." Regular caravan camels traveled about twenty-five miles a day at a speed of about three miles an hour. Some caravans were made up of as many as sixteen hundred camels.

Clothing made of camel's hair meant that the wearer was considered a prophet. Such men were Elijah and John the Baptist.

Camels can drink as much as nine gallons of water at a single drink, and have been known to drink thirty gallons of water in as little as ten minutes. If Rebekah watered ten camels and they each drank thirty gallons of water, she would have had to draw three hundred gallons of water for them!

Share and Compare

1. What is YOUR name in the YOU story?_____

2. Who is YOUR best friend?_____

3. How old was Rebekah in the YOU story?_____

4. What kind of a god did most of the people in the city of Haran worship?_____

   _____

5. Whom did Rebekah and her family worship?_____

6. What did Rebekah believe the Lord would provide for her?_____

7. Write the number of the description in Column 2 by its match in column 1.

a. Bethuel	1. Sent servant to find his son a bride
b. Haran	2. Father of Rebekah
c. Isaac	3. One of the Hebrew names for God
d. Laban	4. New home of Rebekah
e. Jehovah	5. City of moon-god worship
f. Abraham	6. Man Rebekah would marry
g. Caravan	7. Brother of Rebekah
h. Beer-Sheba	8. Group of people and animals who travel together for protection

8. Rebekah offered to carry water for the camels to drink. This meant she had to do a lot of work because the animals were so thirsty. What does that show us about the kind of person she was?

   _____

   Rebekah had no mother-in-law to help her in her new home. Is that important?_____ Why?_____

9. The YOU story used another word that means the same as an engagement or marriage promise. What was that word?_____

10. Read Genesis 24:40. How did Abraham say the Lord would help the servant find a wife for Abraham's son?_____

11. Read Genesis 24:50. Why were Laban and Bethuel willing to let Rebekah go to a strange country and marry a man she had never met?

12. Why do you think Rebekah herself was willing to go right away with Abraham's servant?_____

    What does her example teach us about God?_____

Time to Trust

We often place trust in things without even realizing that we are doing so. Every time you sit down in a chair you are trusting that chair to hold you. We place trust in people. You trust your parents to provide for your needs of food and shelter.

Every day also brings us opportunities to trust God. Each time we trust Him, our faith in Him increases. It's rather like building up "trust muscles." Each time these "muscles" are used, they become stronger.

The Bible is full of stories about people who used their "trust muscles." The beginnings of some of these stories are given for you here. Read each mini-story. Then look up the scripture reference and write or draw a picture of how the person trusted God in each situation.

Young David, the shepherd boy, challenged the wicked giant, Goliath, to fight him. David refused to wear King Saul's armor or use his weapons. Instead he—(I Samuel 17:45-51)

Joshua and the Israelites were fighting against their enemies, the Amorites. They needed to have more daylight in which to finish the battle and defeat these wicked people. Joshua prayed that the sun and moon would stand still and—(Joshua 10:12-14)

The Israelites complained to Moses that the water they had to drink was bitter. Moses—(Exodus 15:25)

Trust Tangle

Rebekah trusted the Lord to take care of her wherever she went. She believed He would provide for all her needs.

How well have you learned the lesson of trust? Trust the openings in the boxes to lead you safely through the tangle and to the memory verse. As you follow the open gates in each square, write the letters in the correct order on the lines below the tangle.

Memorize the verse to gain your reward.

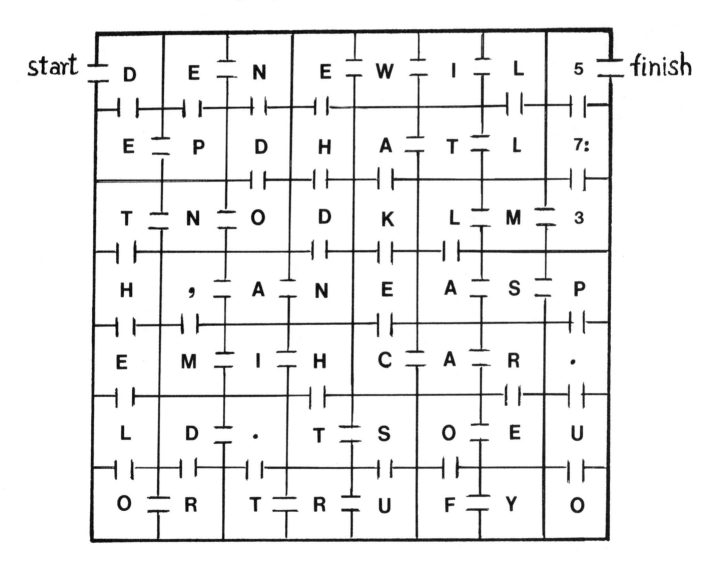

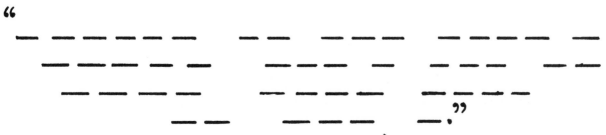

The Mystery of the Silver Cup

GENESIS 44:14-45:15

> YOU are Simri. (SIM-ree)
>   He is the son of the chief steward to Joseph, Grand Vizier of Egypt.

"Hurry, my son, the men are back. Help me prepare the water for washing our guests' feet."

YOU scurry to help YOUR father, who is the steward of Joseph, Grand Vizier of Egypt. "What men do you mean?" YOU ask as YOU put a basin on the table.

"Do you remember my telling YOU about the ten Hebrew brothers who came to buy grain a few months ago?" He reaches for the water pitcher. "The ones our master accused of being spies?"

YOU hold the basin steady as YOUR father pours in the water. "Oh yes, now I remember. Our master put them in prison for three days and then let them go home, didn't he?"

"Not all of them, Simri. Joseph demanded that they leave one brother behind in prison. Then he gave me special instructions about them," YOUR father says, setting down the water pitcher.

YOU giggle as YOU remember the rest of what YOUR father told YOU about these foreigners. "Oh, how I would have loved to see their faces when they found their money put back in their grain sacks!" you say.

YOUR father chuckles. "Then YOU should have been with me just now. They are still trying to figure out how that happened. They even offered to pay me for it again." He looks around cautiously. "But we must not speak so loudly. No one is supposed to know about that. It was a secret order given to me from Master Joseph."

"Why do you think he wanted them to have their money back? And why didn't he just give it to them? I don't understand." You pick up a towel and follow behind your father as he hastens down the marble columned hall. "Was he just playing a trick on them or is it because he

is not an Egyptian and it was some strange custom from his native land?"

"I don't know, Simri. The important thing is that if it were not for Joseph, we would all be starving. His plan to store grain before this famine came has saved our lives and the lives of our neighbors in Canaan. That is why these men have returned to buy more grain. Master Joseph has invited them to eat with him. Go back to the kitchen now and tell them to be ready to serve the meal when I return. Our master will be here by then. And Simri—"

YOU lay the towel over his arm. "Yes, father?"

"Tell them to be sure to have enough food. Their brother in prison has been released to join them."

"All right." YOU turn and start running back down the hall.

"One more thing, Simri," YOUR father calls out. "They have brought their youngest brother, Benjamin, with them this time."

Later, YOU go to the kitchen where the staff is busy cleaning up after the big noon banquet. Only a few hours have passed since the brothers' arrival, but they have already changed things in Joseph's household. YOU listen carefully to the servants' conversation.

"Did you see the master's face when he saw that youngest brother?"

"Yes, Joseph rushed out of the room, and we had to delay serving the meal. Why did he do that?"

"I don't have any idea. It's all a mystery to me."

YOU could tell them that YOU know that Joseph asked YOUR father to bring water to his bedroom so that he could wash his tear-streaked face, but YOU keep quiet.

"It was such a strange meal. The Hebrew men sat apart, staring at each other. They were amazed because of their special seating arrangement. They said that they were seated in order by their ages."

"Then Joseph sent them food from his own

table. But he sent five times as much food to the youngest one as to the others. Why, he couldn't possibly eat it all!"

That night YOU are still puzzling over the day's surprising events.

"YOU should be asleep, Simri. It is past YOUR bedtime."

"Oh, Father. You are home again. Was Master Joseph sick so that he called for you?"

"No, he wanted to talk to me about the Hebrew men."

"Is he going to give them their money back again?"

"Yes, just as before, except—"

"Except what?"

"Except that Joseph has commanded me to place his silver cup into the sack of the one called Benjamin."

"Master Joseph's silver cup? You mean the one he drinks from?"

"Yes, Simri, that very one. But YOU are to tell no one, absolutely no one, about this. Do YOU understand? Now go to sleep."

"Yes, Father." YOU lie down, but YOU can't fall asleep right away. What YOU don't understand are the bewildering events that seem to center on these eleven Hebrew brothers and YOUR master. What is it all about? YOU finally fall asleep still trying to solve the mystery.

"My son, wake up. It's dawn and I want you to go with me on an errand. We are going to catch up with the Hebrew brothers and get back Master Joseph's silver cup."

. . . .

It is now mid-morning. YOU are standing in a dark corner of the throne room where the Hebrew men huddle together before Joseph.

"But, Sir, what more can we say? We have no idea how your cup came to be in our brother's sack."

"Enough!" Joseph shouts. "Only the thief who stole my silver cup will stay to be my slave. The rest of you may go back to your homeland."

One of the men cries out in anguish and throws himself facedown before Joseph. "Sir, please take me instead! I promised our father that the boy would be safe. Our father is old, and if the boy doesn't return with the others, our father will die.

Let me stay and become your slave in exchange for Benjamin."

Joseph suddenly leaps to his feet and shouts, "Clear the room. Everyone must leave except these men."

The room quickly empties amid gasps of surprise. Can this be the same Joseph you have all known and respected? The master who has been so kind to everyone, even the lowest slave? YOU press back into the shadows, tight against the wall. No one can see YOU here. YOU just *have* to stay and find out what will happen next. What does it all mean?

Joseph turns to the eleven brothers, trembling in terror before him. THEN . . .

Read Genesis 45:1b-15 and write/tell the ending to this mysterious story as **You Are There.**

Fascinating Facts

People in ancient Egypt loved to read just as people do today. At the time of Joseph, Egyptians were reading short stories and some of them were even adventures.

Instead of dabbing perfume behind their ears, Egyptian guests, both men and women, wore cones of perfume on the tops of their heads.

Egyptian children in the time of Joseph's sons had toys. Boys played with leather balls and girls had dolls. Children had wooden animal pull toys on wheels. Everyone enjoyed swimming and parades.

Scholars of ancient Egypt had a wonderful knowledge of mathematics. This helped them make a calendar of 365 days with 24 hours in each day, just as we have today.

People called Hyksos ruled Egypt when Joseph lived there. They were foreigners like him. Perhaps this helped them trust him more than the native Egyptians, and made it easier for God to place Joseph in such a position of authority.

Share and Compare

1. In the YOU story, for whom does YOUR father work?_____

2. What secret orders did Joseph give to his steward when the Hebrew brothers made their first trip to Egypt to buy grain?_____
_____

3. When crops do not grow, and people and animals have no food, it is called a famine. Why did the people in Egypt have food during the famine when other people were starving?_____

4. Whom did the Hebrew brothers bring with them on this second trip to Egypt?
_____

5. Read Genesis 43:29-31. Who was Benjamin?_____
_____

   Why do you think Joseph went to his room and cried when he saw him?_____
_____

6. Why were the eleven brothers so amazed at the way they were seated at the table in Joseph's house?_____

7. What did Joseph tell the steward to do with his silver cup?_____
_____

8. Put the following events in the proper time sequence by writing the letter of the statement in the correct numbered blank.

   a. Joseph tells the steward to hide his silver cup.   1. _____
   b. Joseph goes to his room to cry.   2. _____
   c. Benjamin goes with his brothers to Egypt.   3. _____
   d. The eleven brothers eat at Joseph's house.   4. _____
   e. Everyone but the Hebrews is ordered out of the room.   5. _____
   f. The silver cup is found in Benjamin's sack.   6. _____
   g. Joseph puts one brother in prison.   7. _____

9. What was so special about the silver cup?_____

10. What was supposed to happen to the man who stole the silver cup?_____
_____

11. Why do you think Joseph played this trick on his brothers? (hint: see Genesis 45:4)_____

12. Read Genesis 45:7-8. What did Joseph learn about God that helped him forgive his brothers for the terrible thing they had done to him?_____
_____

Forgiveness Finger Puppets

Joseph is a wonderful example to us of love and forgiveness in action. Even though he had been mistreated by his brothers, he did not hold a grudge against them. Instead, he forgave them and helped them in their time of trouble. He was able to do this because of God's love in his own life. He saw how the Lord had taken care of and blessed him in all the hard times of his life in Egypt. Now Joseph used the power and authority God had given him to bless others.

Showing forgiveness to others, especially those who have hurt us, is not so easy to do. Color and cut out the finger puppets and glue the loops together to fit over your fingers. Read the problem on each puppet and then role play how you would show forgiveness in that situation.

glue

Kristin has lots of great new clothes. She laughs at your hand-me-downs. You hear that her parents are getting a divorce and find her crying in the girls' restroom.

glue

glue

Scott is a terrific athlete. He always makes fun of you because you aren't very good in sports. Now he has a broken leg and can't play ball with the team.

glue

Mummy Mystery

When an Egyptian pharaoh died, he was mummified. This meant that the body was preserved by wrapping it in special cloth bandages. Then, along with many treasures, the mummy was placed in a great stone pyramid for protection from thieves.

Special picture writing, called hieroglyphics, was placed on the inner walls of these tombs. This writing often contained magic spells, supposed to help the pharaoh against any danger he might meet in the next world.

Pretend that you are an archaeologist who is exploring a pyramid. See if you can decode this mystery message. You will find that it is an important one that will help you in getting along with others in today's world.

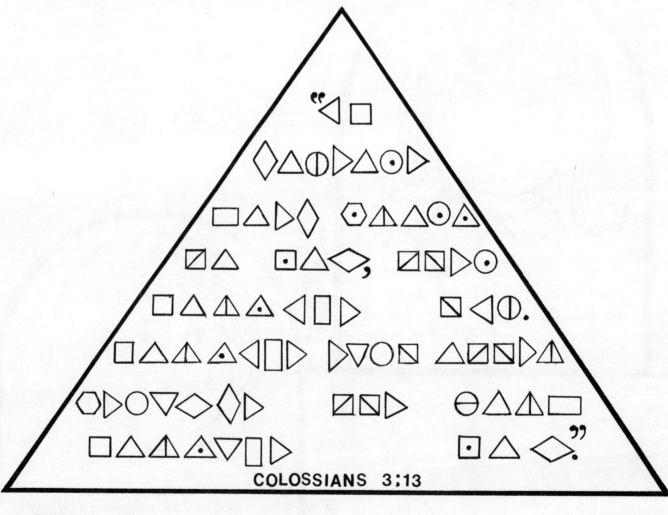

COLOSSIANS 3:13

CODE

Follow the Red Sea Road

Exodus 14:10-31

YOU are Chislon. (CHIS-lun)

He is an Israelite boy caring for his fatherless family as they travel with Moses on the Exodus from Egypt.

"I'm afraid, Chislon. Will the Egyptians kill us like they did Father?" Jesse scoots closer to YOU. YOU can feel his little body shake with fear.

"No!" YOU declare firmly. "The Lord will protect us. It will be all right." YOU try to sound reassuring, hoping YOUR little brother can't hear the panic creeping into YOUR voice. But YOU, too, are afraid. With a shiver YOU recall vividly the horrible scene of YOUR father's death . . .

"I said more bricks and straw, slave." The Egyptian slave master brings his whip down across YOUR father's shoulders. "Your duty is to carry out my commands, not to give me excuses for disobeying orders."

"But, Master, we have gathered all the straw for miles around and there is no more to add to the clay. It just isn't possible to do what you demand," YOUR father says.

"I'll show you what is possible!" the slave master bellows in rage.

YOU'LL never forget that last sight of YOUR father. YOU can still almost feel each blow upon him, beating him down until he lies lifeless on the desert sand. How YOU hate the Egyptians.

And now, here YOU are, with them right behind YOU. On either side of YOU rise steep, barren mountains. And in front of YOU lies the deep, impassible Red Sea. YOU shudder. YOU are cornered. Why did Moses ever bring you Israelites to this awful place anyway? YOUR mother's soft voice brings YOU back to reality.

"Temina is finally asleep, Chislon. With all this traveling by night as well as day, she has her hours all mixed up."

YOU look lovingly at the tiny, curly-haired, baby sister nestled gently in YOUR mother's arms. "She looks just like you, Mother. I wish Father had lived long enough to see her. He would have been so proud of her."

"And he would have been proud of YOU too, Chislon. YOU are doing a good job as the man of our family. We could never make this hard journey if YOU didn't take care of us."

"But what have we accomplished? We are trapped, and the Egyptians are ready to take us all back into slavery. Then they will punish us because of the deaths of their first-born sons. I want to believe Moses, Mother, but what can he be thinking of to bring us here?"

"Have patience with him, Son. YOU know that it took a long time and ten terrible plagues to convince Pharaoh to let us go. The Lord showed us His great power and how much He values us as His people. He is the one who told Moses what to do. He will not forsake Moses, or us, now."

YOU nod. "I'll try. I guess I'm just worried because you three are MY responsibility now. Waiting upon the Lord to help you is the hardest thing of all to do. It's much easier to try to do something yourself."

YOU think about the plagues the Lord brought on the Egyptians. The water in the Nile River turned to blood and all the fish died. No one could drink the water. Then came frogs. They were everywhere and in everything. Lice were next. Swarms of flies then invaded all Egypt except Goshen, where the Israelites lived. Following that, cattle and farm animals became sick and died. Then boils came on all the men and animals.

When terrible hailstones fell and destroyed all the crops in the fields, many of the Egyptian officers had believed Moses and brought their slaves and animals under cover. But everything that was outside was killed. Next came locusts that ate everything that had grown after the hailstorm. They rested at night on the ground in layers four to five inches deep and smelled horrible when stepped on. After that, a thick darkness fell on the Egyptians for three days. In all these plagues, the Lord spared the Israelites from harm and proved that the Egyptian gods were fakes.

Lastly had come the death of all the first-born sons of the Egyptians and their animals. If the Israelites had not obeyed Moses and sprinkled the blood of the Passover lambs on their doorposts, the Lord's death angel would have killed their first-born sons too. That would have meant YOU would have been killed! The Lord may even have placed Moses in this wilderness for forty years to acquaint him with it and prepare him to lead the Israelites through it. Yes, even in this awful predicament, YOU know YOU can trust Moses and the Lord to help YOU.

It's sunset. The pillar of fiery cloud that has led you on your trip has moved. It is no longer in front of you, but now separates the Egyptians from you.

"The Lord says you are not to be afraid. He will save you. The Egyptians you fear will be destroyed. You will never see them again. Only trust the Lord and quietly wait for Him to fight for you."

Then Moses stretches his walking stick out over the sea. Instantly a strong wind comes up from the east. It blows in a straight line across the water, dividing the waves into curls of misty spray on either side of the wind.

"Oh, look," Jesse points at the sea. "There's a path on the water."

"It does sort of look like a path. I wonder what the Lord is doing."

All that night the wind blows strongly. By the light from the fiery pillar, you can see the path becoming more like a road through the sea. Then, while it is still night, Moses commands the Israelites, all two million of them, to follow this Red Sea road.

YOU rouse the sleeping Jesse and round up YOUR few sheep and goats, while YOUR mother arranges the small household articles and divides them in bundles for each of you to carry. Little Temina sleeps soundly, unaware of all the activity around her.

"Are we really going to walk through the water, Chislon?" Jesse rubs his unbelieving eyes with a chubby fist. "Won't we get wet?"

"Moses says the Lord has made it dry for us," YOU encourage him.

YOU can scarcely believe it YOURSELF, but as YOU step into the sea, YOU find that Moses was right. A wide, dry road stretches before YOU with high walls of water towering on either side of it. They extend high above YOUR head like the columns in the great Temple of Amon in Thebes which the Israelites helped to build. But will all of you be able to cross this sea road safely? What about the fierce Egyptian army with their chariots and horses? Won't they use the road also and recapture you? What will happen next? THEN . . .

Read Exodus 14:23-31 and write/tell the overpowering ending to this story as **You Are There.**

Fascinating Facts

Archaeologists have found proof that the Israelites had great difficulty in finding straw to mix with the clay for bricks. They found remains of buildings that showed the lower layers of bricks made with good chopped straw. The next layers had straw stubble that had been pulled up by its roots. The top layers had only clay, with no straw at all.

In the days of the pharaohs, many children died at young ages.

All the boys who were raised in the royal family had to be carefully taught skills in everything in case they might have to become pharaoh some day.

The pharaoh might have several wives, but only one was the queen. And her son became the next king. Because he was believed to be a direct descendant from the gods, this boy-king was married to his sister since no one but his sister would be great enough to be his queen.

A pharaoh was believed to become divine when he was in his royal robes and sitting on his throne. Everything he commanded had to be obeyed because he was the sky god in human form.

Share and Compare

1. In this YOU story, what important position do YOU have?_____
   _____

2. According to the YOU story, why did the Egyptians kill YOUR father?_____

3. In the story, the Israelites were surrounded by several things. Match the obstacles to the correct positions by writing the correct word on each line.
   Behind _____
   Each side _____
   Front _____
   mountains   sea   Egyptians

4. Chislon said it was harder to wait on the Lord to do something for you than to do it yourself. Do you agree?_____
   Explain._____

5. Read Exodus 14:4, 17-18. What does the Lord say will be accomplished by defeating the Egyptians Himself, instead of letting the Israelites gain the victory?_____

6. Each of the plagues is listed below in a scrambled word. Unscramble each word and write the correct word on the line.
   a. The Nile River water turned to (dobol)_____
   b. (Gofrs) were everywhere and in everything._____
   c. (Eilc) were next._____
   d. Swarms of (liefs) invaded everything._____
   e. Cattle and farm animals became (icsk) and (eddi)._____   _____
   f. (Sobil) came on all the men and animals._____
   g. Everything in the fields was killed by (lhainesots)._____   _____
   h. Then (socluts) ate everything green._____
   i. For three days there was a thick (nardekss)._____
   j. An angel (likeld) all the first-born sons of the Egyptians._____

7. Read Exodus 14:10-12. What was the Israelites' reaction to the Egyptians.___

8. What does the answer to question 7 reveal about their relationship to the Lord and Moses?_____

9. Where did the pillar of fiery cloud go?_____

10. What happened when Moses raised his walking stick over the sea?_____

11. According to the YOU story, how many Israelites were there?_____

12. What can we learn from this story? (see Exodus 14:31)_____
    _____

Pop-Up Picture Map

Here is a map of the area the Israelites lived in during their forty years of rebellion and complaining. Some of the problems they encountered are pictured for you. Color the map. Cut along the dotted lines of the pictures and fold up on the solid lines to make a pop-up map.

When you look at your picture-map, remember that in every problem you may have God has promised, "I will never leave you; I will never forget you."—Hebrews 13:5

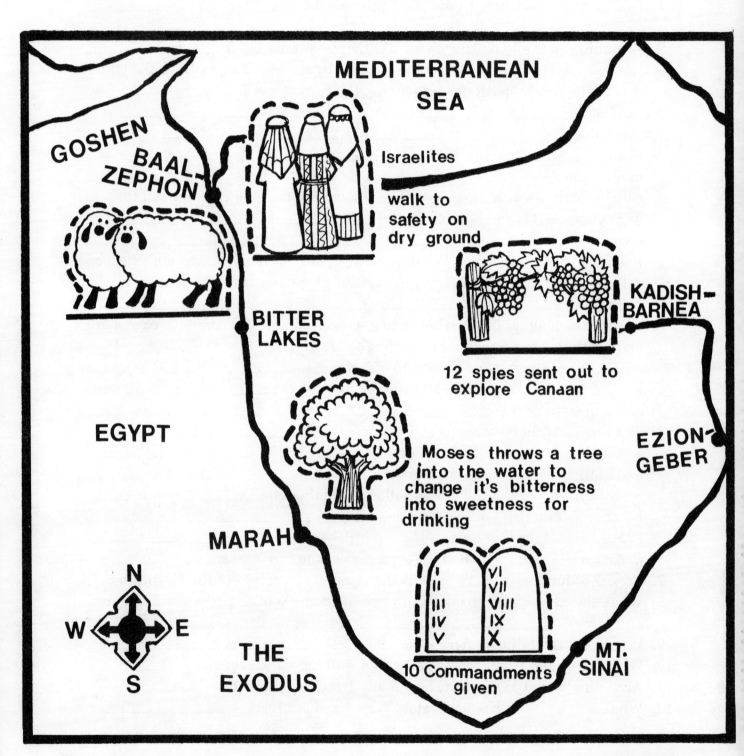

MEDITERRANEAN SEA

GOSHEN

BAAL ZEPHON

Israelites walk to safety on dry ground

KADISH-BARNEA

BITTER LAKES

12 spies sent out to explore Canaan

EGYPT

EZION-GEBER

Moses throws a tree into the water to change it's bitterness into sweetness for drinking

MARAH

N W E S

THE EXODUS

10 Commandments given

MT. SINAI

Wandering Words

Help these Israelite children to find a way through the wilderness to the Promised Land. As you come to the words of the memory verse, write them on the lines provided.

_____

_____

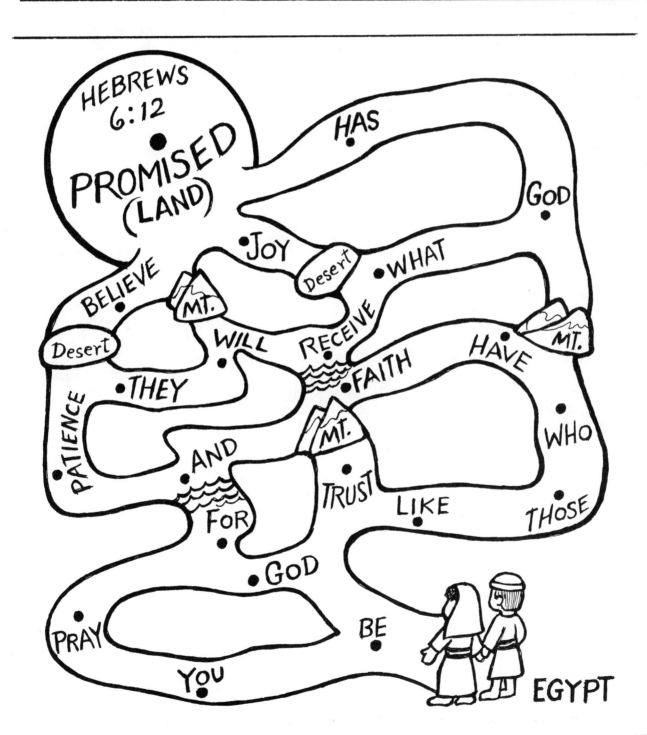

Once More, with Feeling

JOSHUA 6:1-21

> YOU are Asher. (ASH-ur)
> He is an Israelite boy who is a friend of Joshua.

Merab and YOU peek out cautiously from behind a big rock at the bottom of the hill. The city of Jericho looms ahead of you. You bend your necks back, look straight up at the city, and groan.

"It is every bit as big as they said, Asher."

YOU nod sadly at YOUR little sister. "Yes, Jericho is as tall as a mountain. The spies say it has two walls and the gates are tightly locked to keep us outside. They say there is a space between the walls and that the inner wall is twice as thick as the outer wall. Both walls are joined together by houses built in and on top of them."

"How will our army ever be able to conquer such a town?"

YOU remember the answer YOUR friend Joshua gave YOU when YOU asked him that same question. YOU answer YOUR sister the way Joshua answered YOU. "The town is already defeated, Merab."

"But how, Asher?"

"Joshua says he has a secret plan from God."

"Where did he get it?"

YOU sigh. "I don't know, Merab. We'll just have to wait and see."

You both return to camp with more questions than you had when you left.

Early the next morning, the men assemble before Joshua to see what he will do. YOU are not near enough to hear what his orders are, but YOU can see the men in the army look at each other questioningly.

Then YOUR father picks up his spear. He kisses YOUR mother and Merab, and gives YOU a hug. "Goodbye, my loved ones," he says. Then, grim-faced, he marches off.

YOU wave goodbye as long as YOU can see the men. Then the waiting begins. Will YOUR father be hurt or killed in the battle? YOU are really nervous. The camp is surprised to see the army return after only a few hours. No one even seems to be hurt. Priests with their ram's horn trumpets are also with the army. Some of them are even carrying the ark or Holy Box of the Lord. This seems to be a strange battle plan! Well, tomorrow is another day. Perhaps then the Israelite men will take over Jericho.

The next morning, bright and early, the families again wave goodbye. This time surely the Israelites will be victorious. YOU run to the edge of the camp and watch for the signs of battle. There are none! And, in just a little while, YOU see the soldiers and priests all return again. Everyone in camp is puzzled.

"What is Joshua's secret plan, Father?" YOU ask.

He seems uncomfortable, but answers, "I don't want to talk about it. It seems foolish."

Day after day follows in the same way. For six days now the soldiers and priests have gone out of camp, marched once around Jericho, and returned. The men are murmuring about accomplishing nothing. The murmuring increases to muttering and muttering to loud questioning. All through the camp YOU hear discussions of Joshua and his secret plan. "What kind of a plan is this? We well never conquer Jericho this way!"

No one even gets up to see the men off anymore. Each day the soldiers come back looking sheepish and feeling downright foolish. But if the people of Israel feel ridiculous, what do the people of Jericho think about it all?

YOU try to imagine what it is like to be in Jericho these days. At first you would be frightened. You and your family would just wait for the Israelites' attack. If it doesn't come from this march around the walls, it will surely come in the night. The men of the city stay awake all night waiting for the enemy's attack, but there is none.

The next day the enemy again marches

around your city and returns to its camp. Day after day it is the same—the Israelites march but say nothing. There is just the weird sound of their shofars—ram's horn trumpets—bouncing off your walls. What are these crazy Jews up to? YOU imagine that by day six everyone in Jericho would be jumpy and cross from lack of sleep. It would be awful for them.

But now it is day seven. YOU see Joshua get up early and leave YOUR camp. Silently YOU follow him. There he stands, shoulders sagging, looking sad and sort of lonesome as he stares up at the walled city. He is talking to himself.

"We must have this city. It is the gateway to the west. Lord, we have done as You commanded me. Every day the priests have carried Your Holy Box and blown the trumpets. Every day for these six days we have marched silently around this city."

YOU realize then that Joshua is praying.

"Today, You have promised us victory. We wait upon you, O Lord. Give us this city and we will praise You forever."

YOU catch sight of the red-eyed, grumpy people in the city peering out of their windows and rubbing the sleep from their eyes.

Joshua looks at the people in Jericho too and then at the heavens where the sun is turning the clouds pink and gold. He smiles. He turns to leave and sees YOU. He holds out his hand, "Come, Asher. This is our day of triumph." Together YOU and Joshua walk back to camp.

As soon as Joshua arrives, he gives the order to assemble the soldiers and priests. They shuffle into lines and wait, heads hanging, to hear what Joshua has to say.

"Men of Israel, today the Lord has given us this city of Jericho. Today we will fight and victory is ours."

A cheer arises and its echo sounds through the camp. "It is time!"

Now the families catch the excitement. YOU are busy helping YOUR father prepare for battle. YOUR little sister watches wonderingly.

"It is God who has given Joshua this plan, Merab," YOU tell her. "It doesn't have to be explained. God brought us from Egypt and through the wilderness safely. We can trust Him to help us now."

YOU tag along behind the army. YOU are back just far enough to not be noticed. YOU hide behind the big rock again and watch. Joshua says this is the day of victory. We are to give glory to God. What is about to happen? YOU feel YOU will burst with curiosity as YOU watch the army and priests march around Jericho. Then they march around a second time and a third time. YOU count the times they circle around the walled city—four, five, six. No sound is heard but the wail of the shofars. THEN . . .

Read Joshua 6:15-20 and write/tell the surprising end to this story as **You Are There.**

Fascinating Facts

Jericho is considered by some archaeologists to be the oldest city in the world. The walls of Jericho surrounded a land area of about seven or eight acres.

The outer walls rose up from the hillside about thirty to thirty-five feet into the air. This is a bit taller than a three-story building. These walls were six feet thick. The inner walls were about twelve feet thick and even higher! A space of fifteen feet separated the two walls.

There is much geological evidence to point to a massive earthquake occurring in the city. This may have been the method the Lord used to destroy Jericho. Archaeologists have found evidence that when the walls collapsed, the outer wall fell outward. This dragged the inner wall, and the houses built across the top of it and the outer wall, out and down the hill.

Joshua's name and Jesus' name mean the same thing—"Jehovah is salvation." As Joshua led God's people into the Promised Land, so Jesus leads God's people into the Heavenly Kingdom.

Share and Compare

1. In the YOU story, who is YOUR friend?_____

2. Joshua gave a reason in the YOU story why it was important to conquer Jericho. What was that reason_____

3. What did Jericho have that made it such a hard town to conquer?_____
   _____

4. In the YOU story, what did the people of Israel think about Joshua's orders to the soldiers and priests?_____
   Why do you think they felt this way?_____
   _____

5. Where did Joshua get the plan to conquer Jericho?_____
   Does that make a difference?_____ Explain._____
   _____

6. Read Joshua 6:1-21. Write the names of the people who are NOT mentioned in the Bible, on the line below.

   Mother   Asher   soldiers   Father   Joshua   priests   Merab
   townspeople of Jericho

   _____

7. How many days were the Israelites to silently march around the city of Jericho?_____

8. What do you think the people in Jericho thought about what the Israelites were doing?_____
   Why?_____

9. What were the people of Israel to do on the seventh day of Joshua's secret plan?
   _____

10. Read Joshua 6:16. Joshua gives the people the reason they are all to shout. What is that reason?_____

11. Read Joshua 6:2. What made Joshua able to stand firm in carrying out God's plan for Jericho?_____

12. What does Joshua's example in this story teach us about God?_____
    _____

Obedience Originals

There are many examples throughout the Bible of people who, through obedience, became blessings to others. We might call each of them "Thumbody Special." Look up the reference and write in the name of the obedient person on the line below it.

Now you can make "Thumbodies" with your thumb and a stamp pad. Press your thumb onto the stamp pad. Make a thumbprint on the paper by each Bible reference. This will make a base for a picture. You can then have fun by drawing "Thumbody" people out of each print. See if you can make them look like the persons for whom they stand.

Acts 10:19, 20

_____

1 Samuel 3:10

_____

Genesis 12:1, 2

_____

Esther 7:13

_____

Genesis 7:5

_____

Acts 9:4, 6

_____

Exodus 6:10, 11

_____

Judges 7:15

_____

Joshua 6:17

_____

Obedience Orbit

An "orbit" is a regular path traveled by someone, or something, around an object. When Joshua and the Israelites obeyed God, they made an orbit around Jericho once each day for six days. Then, on the seventh day, they made seven orbits around Jericho.

Here is an orbit puzzle for you to solve. It contains a verse that will be helpful to you in those times when obedience to the Lord is not exciting. Memorize it to use against Satan when problems seem overwhelming.

Write down EVERY OTHER letter in the blanks below the puzzle. Make TWO orbits around the scripture reference so that all the letters are used.

PSALM 119:166

" ___ ___ ___ ___ ___ ___ ___ ___ ___

___ ___ ___ , ___ ___ . ___ ___ ___ ___

___ ___ ___ ___ ___ . "

Just One More Chance

JUDGES 16:17-31

> YOU are Irijah. (ih-RIE-juh)
> He is a Gentile boy, who has been captured and taken from his home by the Philistines. He is a slave in their palace and becomes a friend to Samson.

"Irijah!" Zephon bellows. "Where are you, Slave?"

"Coming, Master." YOU sprint around the corner and crash into the furious palace steward.

He grabs YOU by the ear and slaps YOUR face hard. "It's about time YOU showed up, YOU worthless pig."

YOU cry out. Tears well up in YOUR eyes and run down YOUR stinging cheeks.

"The king wants to have that blind prisoner brought to the temple immediately," Zephon fumes.

"Samson?" YOU ask, squirming painfully under his hand hold.

"Yes, the one and only. As if I didn't have more than enough to do already with the harvest celebration. Now, I have to waste my time fetching a helpless captive to amuse a crowd of drunken fools!" Zephon releases YOU and shoves YOU roughly in the direction of that part of the palace where the prisoners are kept. "Now, be quick about it," he says. "See that YOU deliver that miserable vermin to the temple at once or YOU'LL feel more than a mere cuff on the cheek for YOUR disobedience."

YOU stumble down the dark, sunless hallway in a daze. YOU wipe some tears off YOUR cheek with the back of YOUR hand. Samson. What are they going to do to him now? Haven't they done enough already?

YOU think back to the first time YOU saw Samson—a massive mountain of a man—head shaved—blood streaming down his face—empty holes where his eyes had been torn out. His hands were fastened with heavy bronze chains to the huge millstone used to grind grain for the royal court. There he walked, around and around in an endless circle of choking dust while the Philistine kings and officers jeered. "Where is your strength now, O Boaster of Jehovah?"

YOU had felt a sympathy and oneness with this humiliated captive. YOU, too, were far from YOUR home and family—a helpless slave in a strange land. YOU had washed his face and tried to make him comfortable. "Come, Samson. You need to eat and then rest," YOU had urged. But it was in vain. It had taken a long time before he had let YOU help him. At first he would only knock the bowl of food from YOUR hand or turn his back on YOU.

When he thought he was alone he would talk to himself. "I am a fool. How could I ever think I could trust her? Hadn't Delilah shown me over and over she really cared nothing about me? O, Jehovah, how could I have wasted the strength and ability You gave me in such a way as that? O, my Lord, forgive me my sins. Forgive me and restore me to Your love again!"

As Samson learned to trust YOU, he taught YOU about his God, Jehovah. "The Lord is the one who made everything, Irijah. He is the only true God. He loves us no matter what we have done."

YOU had cringed, remembering the honey cake YOU stole from Zephon when he wasn't looking. "Even when we have sinned, Samson?"

His look had been full of pain. "Even when we have sinned."

"And can He forgive us too?"

He had been silent for a moment. Then he nodded reassuringly. "Yes, Little One. He can even forgive us when we confess our sins to Him."

"What does 'confess' mean, Samson?"

"It means to agree with the Lord that we have done wrong, Irijah. To be so sorry for doing it that we won't do it any longer." He had smiled at YOU. "Then Jehovah will forgive us and answer our prayers again."

YOU remember that as Samson had shared

his God with YOU, his faith was made strong again. His physical blindness only increased his inward vision of the Lord and His mercy and forgiveness.

. . . .

"Who's there?"

YOU are suddenly brought back to the world around YOU and find YOURSELF standing in the doorway of Samson's prison cell. The stone floor chills YOUR bare feet and works its way up YOUR body until it reaches YOUR heart. There it seems to settle with a numbing cold that not even the hottest sun could thaw. YOUR eyes adjust to the darker gloom of the prison and YOU see a rat scurry across the floor, its claws scratching on the stones. This is a horrid place for a man to be. "It's just me, Irijah," YOU say shivering.

A man rouses himself and comes out of the shadows. "It is good to hear your voice, Boy. How are YOU today? Is it, is it a sunny day?" His voice is wistful.

"Yes, Samson. It's a sunny day." YOU brush the remaining tears away.

"What brings YOU here with such sadness in your voice, Irijah?"

"You are to be brought to the temple of Dagon at once, Samson," YOU say, striving to keep YOUR voice from breaking. "The king has sent for you to be presented at the harvest festival." YOU step close so he can put a hand on YOUR shoulder to help himself up. The heavy chains clank as he struggles to his feet.

YOU take Samson's hand and lead him through the maze of halls, across the courtyard, and into the temple. He is strangely silent. As YOU glance up at him YOU can see he is deep in thought. He runs his hand through his long hair. Then he prays quietly. "Lord God, give me back my strength. Give me just one last chance to honor You."

What does Samson mean? What has he got in mind?

As soon as you enter the temple you can hear the coarse laughter of the worshipers as they catch sight of the once mighty man of God. Taunts arise from every direction as there are people on the roof as well as in the hall itself.

Samson stumbles on an uneven stone and YOU reach out to steady him.

"What's the matter, Samson?" scoffs the king.

"Can't you see where you are going?"

"Irijah, lead me to the center pillars that hold up the roof. I want to lean against them," Samson says.

YOU place one of his hands on each of the two pillars. "Here, Samson."

"Now, Irijah, get out of this temple at once."

"But, Samson—."

"Don't talk, Boy, just do as I say. Run! And the Lord bless YOU!"

YOU do as Samson orders and race out of the temple. Only when YOU are outside in the courtyard do YOU turn around to look back. THEN . . .

Read Judges 16:30-31 and write/tell the triumphant ending to this almost tragic story as **You Are There.**

Fascinating Facts

Samson was the strongest man who ever lived. Once he killed a lion with his bare hands. He killed one thousand Philistines at one time with the jawbone of a donkey. He humiliated the people of Gaza by carrying off their city's two gate doors and doorposts, thirty-eight miles away. Since the gates were the symbols of the strength of the city, this was a great embarrassment to the people of Gaza.

On another occasion, Samson caught three hundred foxes and tied them in pairs by their tails. He attached torches to their tails and set them on fire. Then he released them into the fields and orchards of his enemies so that the fire burned up their crops.

The Philistines were enemies of Israel for about two hundred years. The secret of their power was that they knew how to work with iron and could make swords, spears, and chariots for war that were too strong for their enemies.

Samson wore his long hair arranged into seven braids.

Paul Anderson, an outspoken Christian weight lifter, held the record and title of "World's Strongest Man" for many years.

Share and Compare

1. What is YOUR name in the YOU story?_____

2. In the YOU story, who is YOUR friend?_____

3. Write the number of the description in Column 2 by its match in Column 1.

    a. Dagon _____   1. The palace steward

    b. Zephon _____   2. People who were enemies of Israel

    c. Philistines _____   3. A slave boy

    d. Samson _____   4. A false god of the Philistines

    e. Irijah _____   5. Woman who betrayed Samson

    f. Delilah _____   6. Israclite judge – strongest man who ever lived

4. What special occasion was going on at the temple?_____
_____

5. Read Judges 16:17. What was the source of Samson's strength?
_____

6. In the YOU story, the first time YOU see Samson his head has been shaved. Does this have anything to do with his becoming a prisoner?_____ Explain.
_____

7. What did the Philistines make Samson do in prison?_____
_____

8. In the YOU story, Samson gave Irijah a definition of what CONFESS means. What was that definition?_____

9. According to Judges 16:27, how many people were on the temple roof?_____

10. How was Samson able to push the pillars down? (see Judges 16:22, 28)_____
_____

11. What might have been one reason God helped Samson tear down the temple and kill the Philistines? (hint: see Judges 16:23, 24)_____
_____

12. Read Samson's prayer in Judges 16:28. Does this show us anything about his attitude toward God?_____
Explain._____

Confession Cartoon

When Samson confessed his sins of foolishness and sinful pride to the Lord, God forgave him and answered his prayer. He gave Samson one more chance to prove that he really did love and serve Him.

Another person in the Old Testament who had to confess his sins was the king of Nineveh. When Jonah preached to the people who lived in Nineveh, he told them that the Lord was going to destroy their city in forty days because of their great wickedness. All the people confessed their sins and showed God just how sorry they really were about their wrong deeds.

In Jonah 3:6-10 read what the king of Nineveh did to show God he was sorry for his sins. Use the spaces below to draw a cartoon illustrating what the king did.

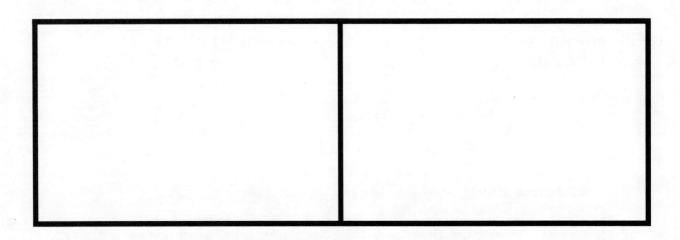

Think of something that you need to confess to the Lord. Use these spaces to draw a cartoon showing how you might show God that you are sorry for that sin. Don't forget to write any words you might say in word balloons similar to those used in cartoon strips.

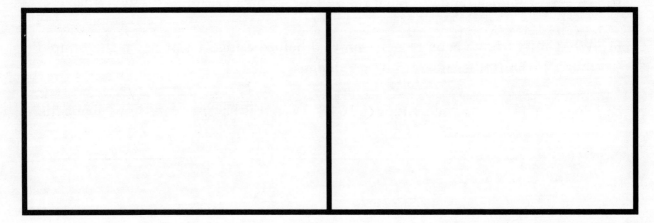

Reverse Rewrite

The dictionary in the International Children's Bible says that the word repent means "being sorry for doing something wrong and not continuing to do that wrong thing. It is to change your heart and life."

Samson made just that kind of a change in his heart and life. It could be said that Samson made a U turn in his life. He made a complete turn around—away from the wrong things he had been doing and toward the right things of the Lord's will.

In the New Testament, the apostle Peter told Jewish people to do the same thing in their lives. He told them about Jesus and what to do about their sins.

See if you can discover just what Peter told these people by rewriting the verse found on this page. Rewrite the verse as it should be on the lines below it. (clue: the title of this activity will help you)

91:3 STCA

"SNIS RUOY EVIGROF LLIW EH DNA

DOG OT KCAB EMOC

!SEVIL DNA STRAEH RUOY

EGNAHC TSUM UOY"

_____

_____

_____

_____

_____

Follow That Arrow

I Samuel 20:17-42

YOU are Hesed. (HUH-said)

He is the personal slave of Prince Jonathan, son of King Saul of Israel. His family are also slaves to the royal family.

YOU cover YOUR ears to muffle the blasts of the shofars. The priests announce the Feast of the New Moon by blowing these ceremonial ram's horn trumpets.

"I don't care if they can only play two notes on them. The shofars hurt my ears, Hesed," Reu says, and grimaces, uncovering his ears.

"The feast is worth a minor earache, Reu," YOU answer, laughing. "We will have roasted, fatted lambs and stall-fed calves, extra bread and fruit."

"Don't forget the honeycakes. And YOU are right, Hesed. Not only is the food delicious, but the day off from work is worth twice the discomfort of the shofar's noise."

YOU and YOUR best friend, Reu, are both slaves in the royal household of King Saul. YOUR master is Prince Jonathan, the next in line to be king of Israel. Reu belongs to the great musician and warrior, David.

The first day of the feast passes all too quickly. The second day YOU are kept busy with YOUR family until it is time for the banquet. That's when YOU find YOUR friend again.

"Oh, there you are, Reu. I've been looking all over for you. Where have you been? C'mon, let's eat our meal together."

"I'm sorry, Hesed. I've been searching for Master David. I didn't want to miss his singing and playing at the festival. He wasn't at the king's table yesterday, and it seems no one has seen him today either."

"That's strange. Whenever the king is sad, David plays the harp and sings for him. It always seems to make Saul feel better. That is, it

used to make him feel better. Do you remember what happened the last time David played for the king?"

"I sure do!" Reu answers. "Saul's knuckles turned white as he clutched the spear he held. Suddenly he leaped to his feet and threw the spear. It sped straight toward David!"

"It was scary. The people all panicked. The spear stuck, quivering, in the wall right behind where David had been sitting only a moment before. Prince Jonathan hurried David out of the room while the people quieted Saul."

"Well, David hasn't been seen since then."

YOU think back to when David first came to live at the king's court. Prince Jonathan had loved David as a blood brother from the first day he met him. He had given David his princely robe, tunic, sword, bow, and belt. Everyone had gasped and whispered as Jonathan had helped David into the royal clothes. They had understood it meant that Jonathan was giving up the position of future king. He was showing the people that he believed David should be raised to that important job. King Saul had begun to be jealous of David. Now he openly called David his enemy.

YOU and Reu get your food and sit down where you can see the king and Prince Jonathan at the royal table. King Saul keeps looking from David's empty chair to Jonathan and back at the chair again. Finally, he asks the question YOU and others are thinking.

"Why hasn't David come to the meal either yesterday or today?"

The people stop talking and turn toward Jonathan. They want to hear his answer too.

The prince looks straight into the king's eyes. "David earnestly asked me for permission to go to Bethlehem to celebrate there with his own family."

Saul pounds his fists on the table and stamps his feet. His face is the color of the pomegranates at harvest. "Don't I know that you have sided with the son of Jesse? As long as he lives on this earth, neither you nor your kingdom will be established. Now send and bring David to me, for he must die!"

YOU are terrified because YOU know that now Saul is not only furious with David, but also with YOUR beloved master, Jonathan. The king lunges savagely forward and hurls his spear at his very own son. The spear misses its mark and Jonathan stalks indignantly out of the room.

All the rest of the day is like a nightmare. YOU stay near Prince Jonathan, just in case YOU might be needed. How awful it must be for him, loving two people who are enemies of each other. And what is even worse, those two are his father and his best friend. To which one should he be loyal? The prince refuses to eat for the rest of the day. That night his lamp is still burning when YOU finally curl up on a mat near his bed and drop off into a troubled sleep. And when the prince awakens YOU, it seems that YOU have not slept at all.

"Come, Hesed, let us go practice some archery."

YOU jump up and hurry to get his bow and arrows. The sun is just peeking over the tree-tops as you reach the field outside the town. Jonathan often practices here. There is a big stone in the middle of the field. Sometimes the prince sets up small targets near it and then sees how close he can come to the stone without hitting it.

The prince fits his arrow onto the string and pulls it back almost to his nose. There is a loud "twang" as the string is released and the arrow skims through the air.

"Run, Hesed. Find the arrow I shot."

YOU run as fast as YOU can, being careful not to stumble on the uneven ground. YOU have lost sight of the arrow, but Jonathan shouts instructions.

"Isn't the arrow beyond you? Hurry! Go quickly! Don't stop!"

YOU catch sight of the arrow and carefully pull it out of the dirt. YOU are careful not to ruin the feathers which guide its direction. Wait a minute. What is that strange shadow?

For a moment it looked like a man hiding behind the stone. Now YOU can't see it. It must just have been YOUR tired, sleepy eyes and the morning sun playing tricks on YOU.

YOU hurry back to Jonathan. "Here is the arrow, Master."

He hands YOU his bow and the quiver of arrows. "Go, Hesed, and carry these back to town."

The prince stays behind in the field. YOU jog off, but turn around to see if he is all right. YOU are worried. It isn't like Jonathan to shoot only one arrow and then quit.

What YOU see causes YOU to stop dead still. YOU rub your eyes in disbelief. Can it be? THEN...

Read 1 Samuel 20:41-42 and write/tell the emotion-packed ending of this story as **You Are There.**

Fascinating Facts

In the time of David, most Israelite soldiers used bows and arrows as weapons. Jonathan belonged to the tribe of Benjamin. This tribe was especially known for its skill with this weapon. Archers sometimes dipped the points of their arrows in poison. At other times the arrows were wound with cord and pitch and set on fire. To protect themselves from these fiery arrows, soldiers would soak their leather shields in water. These wet shields then put out the fire when the arrows stuck in them.

All by himself, Jonathan killed all the Philistines who guarded a valley south of Michmash.

In Bible times, beautiful robes of fine materials were given to people to indicate authority or power. If an official's elaborate outer robe was removed from him, it meant he was fired from his job.

Share and Compare

1. What is a shofar?_____

   What is it used for in this YOU story?_____

2. In this YOU story, who are YOU?_____

3. Write the number of the description in Column 2 by its match in Column 1.

   a. Reu _____   1. Servant to Jonathan
   b. Saul _____   2. Musician
   c. Jonathan _____   3. King of Israel
   d. Hesed _____   4. Slave belonging to David
   e. David _____   5. Son of the king

4. What did David do for King Saul?_____

5. What did Saul try to do to David?_____

6. According to the YOU story, what was Prince Jonathan trying to show the people by giving his royal clothing and weapons to David?_____
   _____

7. Read 1 Samuel 20:17-42. Put the following events in the proper time sequence by writing the letter of the statement in the correct numbered blank.

   a. David hid in the field.   1. _____
   b. Saul tried to kill Jonathan.   2. _____
   c. The Feast of the New Moon is celebrated.   3. _____
   d. Jonathan told David of a secret plan to warn him about Saul.   4. _____
   e. Jonathan told his servant to find the arrows.   5. _____
   f. King Saul asked Jonathan about David.   6. _____

8. What was the secret signal that Jonathan used to let David know Saul wanted to kill him? (see 1 Samuel 20:22)_____
   _____

9. Read 1 Samuel 20:24. Where was David during the feast?_____
   _____

10. Why did Saul want to kill David? (see 1 Samuel 20:31)_____
    _____

11. How did Jonathan feel about David?_____

    How do you know this?_____

12. Would you like to have a friend like Jonathan?_____

    Explain._____

Companion Cablegrams

The friendship that Jonathan and David shared made them close companions in many happy adventures. They enjoyed each other and cried when they knew they could never be together again because of Saul's hatred of David.

Good friends like to spend time together. When they can't be with each other in person, they call or write to say how they miss each other.

On each of these cablegrams, write a short message of friendship from one Biblical person to another. Remember that cablegrams should be limited to ten words or less!

MID-EASTERN UNION

To: Orpah
Message:

From: Ruth

Scripture reference: Ruth 1:3-5, 14-18

MID-EASTERN UNION

To: Ethiopian Eunuch
Message:

From: Philip

Scripture reference: Acts 8:27-30, 35-39

MID-EASTERN UNION

To: Nehemiah
Message:

From: King Artaxerxes

Scripture reference: Nehemiah 2:1-7

MID-EASTERN UNION

To: Priscilla and Aquila
Message:

From: Apollos

Scripture reference: Acts 18:24-27

Active Arrows

Jonathan did more than tell his friend, David, how much he loved him. He showed it in many different ways. Every day we show people what we think about them by the way we act toward them.

You can tell your mom, "I love you." It's much harder to demonstrate that love by volunteering to wash the dishes or clean up your room.

The active arrows in this puzzle will reveal a Bible verse that helps us with this common problem.

DIRECTIONS:

Follow the active arrows in the puzzle to find the next letter. Then write the letters in the blanks below the puzzle to form the words of this memory verse.

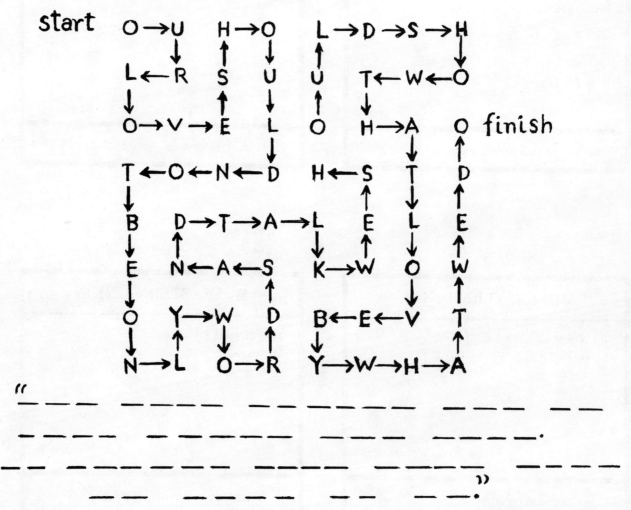

1 JOHN 3:18

The Contest

I KINGS 18:20-39

YOU are Lael. (LAY-ul)

She is an Israelite girl who serves the one true God, Jehovah. She trusts Elijah as God's prophet.

"Perida! Perida! Have you heard the news?" YOU narrowly miss colliding head first with YOUR cousin at the corner of her house.

"What news is that, Lael?" she asks.

"Elijah is back."

"Oh, that. Yes. I also heard that King Ahab called him the biggest troublemaker in Israel, and I agree."

YOU wince. "Perida, how can you say that? Why, Elijah is the servant of Jehovah. He is the one who brings us the Lord's word."

"He does, does he?" Perida challenges defiantly, hands on her hips. "Well, all he has brought so far is hunger and death by this great drought. For three and one-half years now, we haven't had a drop of rain or even dew. There are no crops. The water is gone. People and animals are dying everywhere."

"But that was only to prove to King Ahab that the Lord, not Baal, is the one who gives rain and causes everything to grow."

"Well, it was a poor way to prove his point. All YOUR Elijah did was to cause more child sacrifices to Baal—the very thing Elijah says he hates. Was that Jehovah's will?" Perida is furious.

YOU hate to have these arguments with her. "Oh, Perida, no! It's never the Lord's will to see such cruelty and murder. He never demanded that babies be burned alive on an altar. You know that. It was the prophets of Baal and Asherah. Just like they told your parents to..."

(Oh no! YOU promised never to talk about that.)

"Told them to do what, Lael? Come on—out with it." Perida's eyes pierce right through YOU.

"Just like they told your parents to kill their firstborn baby and ... and ..." YOU choke. "And build his body into the wall of your house as a sacrifice to Baal, so he would bless your family."

Perida is stunned. "That can't be true. YOU'RE just making that up. My parents worship at Baal's temple at the Celebration of the New Year, but they would never do that." She bursts into tears.

YOU try to put your arms around her. "I'm so sorry. It was before you were born. My parents told me about it."

She stiffens and bitterly pushes YOU away. "That was a horrid thing to say. You might as well call my parents, and the prophets of Baal, murderers. Now, get out of here. I hate you!"

Sadly YOU turn away and go home.

"I didn't even get to tell her that Elijah has commanded everyone to meet with him on Mt. Carmel, Mother. She was so angry she wouldn't listen to me."

YOUR mother lays her hand gently on YOUR shoulder. "Not angry, Lael. She was hurt and upset. It must have been a great shock to hear about it from YOU like that. But I can understand why her parents haven't told her."

YOU sigh. "Why do they worship Baal, anyway? It only separates our family."

"There are very few Israelites who haven't joined King Ahab and Queen Jezebel in this awful idolatry. Perhaps now that Elijah has returned, things will be different. We must just keep on praying for Perida and her family."

The next day everyone goes to the meeting with Elijah. Two sacrificial bulls stand in a clearing. King Ahab stands on one side of them with the four hundred and fifty prophets of Baal and the four hundred prophets of Asherah, all impressive in ceremonial robes. Elijah stands alone on the other side, straight and silent, in a leather loincloth and hairy animal-hide cloak. His face is stern and very serious.

YOU look around and see Perida and her family near you. YOU slip over to her. "I'm glad to see you, Cousin. I'm sorry I hurt your feelings yesterday."

Just then, Elijah holds up his hand for silence and declares loudly, "It is time for you Israelites to make a decision. You have been serving both the Lord and Baal. Today, I will prove to you who is the true God. You prophets of Baal and Asherah, build an altar and lay firewood on it. Take one of the bulls. Kill it, and cut it into pieces. Put it on your altar, but don't light a fire. I will do the same thing with the other bull. Then we will each pray to our gods. Whichever god answers the prayer with fire will prove that he is the true God."

Perida gives YOU a look of scorn. "Now we will see who is right, Lael," she sneers. "YOUR great prophet looks like he is going to need lots of help. I'm willing to worship whoever proves himself to be God. What about YOU? Are YOU willing to do the same?"

Why does she have to act like this? "Yes, I am willing. I know that it will be Jehovah," YOU gulp. YOU realize that YOUR life may be at stake, because Queen Jezebel has killed many who believe in the Lord.

Time passes slowly. The prophets of Baal dance around and around their altar until noon. Elijah begins to make fun of them. "Perhaps you should pray louder. Maybe Baal is thinking, or busy, or traveling. Why, he might even be sleeping, so you will have to wake him!"

The prophets pray louder. Then they begin to cut themselves with spears and swords. Their beautiful robes are stained with the blood that flows down their backs, chests, and arms. Their dancing is wilder and the music and chanting is deafening. But no matter what they do, there is no answer from Baal. There is only a heavy silence and stifling heat as the crowd watches, wide-eyed, and dry-mouthed to see what will happen. The people are hot and weary, but no one dares to leave this contest.

Then, at last, the sun begins to set. It is time for the evening sacrifice. Elijah gathers the people around him and places the sacrificial bull on the stone altar he has built. There are twelve stones, one for each of the twelve tribes of Israel. A ditch is dug around the altar. Elijah orders the people to fill four jars with water and pour them over the altar. YOU can almost taste that wonderful water as it sloshes over the meat and wood. Unbelievably, Elijah orders the same thing to be done two more times. Twelve jars of water have now soaked the sacrifice and filled the ditch surrounding the altar. Tension is high as Elijah turns toward the altar.

YOU hold YOUR breath. What will happen next? Will the Lord really answer with fire and prove He is the true God? He just has to! THEN ...

Read 1 Kings 18:36-40 and write/tell the incredible ending to this story as **You Are There.**

Fascinating Facts

A statue of a calf was often used to symbolize the idol Baal. He was the god who supposedly brought rain and made the crops grow. His wife, Ashtoreth, was the goddess of fertility. Temples to both of these false deities were usually built side by side, or one temple housed both gods.

Part of the worship of these idols included kissing their images and the burning of an eternal flame before them. There was a great deal of sexual sin included in this worship also. This, plus the fact of the legalized murder of infants as sacrifices, was against the laws that the Lord gave to the Israelites.

When Jehu became king of Israel, he completely destroyed the temple of Baal and killed the remaining priests and followers in the temple itself. Then he turned the temple and its courtyard into a public toilet. Perhaps this was the only fitting use for such a facility which had been dedicated to sin and evil!

Share and Compare

1. In this YOU story, whom do YOU worship?_____
2. Who is Perida?_____
3. Why are YOU always arguing with her?_____
4. This YOU story told some of the things that people did when they worshiped Baal. Name some of these._____

   _____

5. Do the answers to question 4 make a difference in how we understand Elijah's harsh treatment of the prophets of Baal in 1 Kings 18:40?_____ Explain.

   _____

6. Put the following events in the proper time sequence by writing the letter of the statement in the correct numbered blank.

   a. Elijah builds an altar and places firewood and meat on it.   1. _____
   b. There is no rain or dew for three and one-half years.   2. _____
   c. Elijah makes fun of the prophets of Baal.   3. _____
   d. Elijah returns.   4. _____
   e. The Lord sends fire to burn up Elijah's sacrifice.   5. _____
   f. The prophets of Baal cut themselves with swords and spears.   6. _____
   g. The prophets of Baal build an altar and place firewood and   7. _____
      meat on it.

7. Where did the great contest take place?_____
8. Read 1 Kings 18:27. What were some of the things that Elijah said Baal might be doing instead of answering the prophets' prayers?_____

   _____

9. How many stones did Elijah use to build the altar to the Lord?_____ Why did he choose that number of stones?_____
10. Why do you think Elijah had the people pour water over the altar until it filled the ditch surrounding it?_____
11. Read 1 Kings 18:36-37. In his prayer, what things did Elijah ask the Lord to do?

   _____

12. What lesson can we learn from this story of Elijah?_____

   _____

Christian Connections

The names of many famous Christians are hidden in this crossword puzzle. Read the clues and fill in the names of each person. (Hint: Each of the LAST NAMES of the people listed below has a place in this puzzle.)

ACROSS

1. first American woman doctor
4. missionary martyred by Auca Indians in Ecuador
7. Apache Indian chief converted six years before his death
8. "Father of the Protestant Reformation"
9. wrote the book *Pilgrim's Progress*
10. helped found the American Sunday School Union and wrote the "Star Spangled Banner"
11. space shuttle commander whose recorded personal testimony of faith in Jesus Christ was broadcast into Communist lands
12. southern "colonel" who founded fast-food restaurant chain
13. missionary who was first white woman to cross the Rockies

DOWN

2. 1924 Olympic medal winner who refused to race on Sundays
3. U. S. Secretary of Treasury who placed "In God We Trust" on coins
5. burned as a martyr for translating the Bible into English
6. evangelist who started Bible Institute and publishing firm—published first paperback books
7. first gospel artist to receive gold album from recording industry of America
9. founder of the Salvation Army
10. black minister who led Civil Rights marches

SALMON CHASE

JIM ELLIOT

JOHN BUNYAN

FRANCIS SCOTT KEY

MARTIN LUTHER KING, Jr

NARCISSA WHITMAN

HARLAN SANDERS

DWIGHT L. MOODY

WILLIAM TYNDALE

GERONIMO

ERIC LIDDELL

AMY GRANT

JACK LOUSMA

MARTIN LUTHER

ELIZABETH BLACKWELL

WILLIAM BOOTH

Counting Commitment

A commitment is a promise or a pledge to someone. Elijah made a commitment to the Lord when he promised to serve Him faithfully. He pledged himself to show the Israelites, once and for all, who was the true God by this contest against the prophets of Baal.

Here are some words taken from the story. Add or subtract letters in the order given to find a hidden word to fit the blanks. (You also have to unscramble some of them.) Then write these words on the lines below the puzzle so they will form a Scripture verse about commitment.

LAEL − A + O + V − L = ___ ___ ___ ___

IT + H + E − I = ___ ___ ___

MOTHER + D − M + L − TH − E = ___ ___ ___ ___

HURRY − H + Y + O − RY = ___ ___ ___ ___

STONES − ES + D − ST + G − N = ___ ___ ___

WORSHIP − O + I − RS + T − IP = ___ ___ ___ ___

SADLY − S − D + L − Y = ___ ___ ___

YEAR − E + O − A + U = ___ ___ ___ ___

SERVANT − S + H − RV − N + R = ___ ___ ___ ___ ___

TALK − K + L − T = ___ ___ ___

WATER − W + Y − A + O − T + U − E = ___ ___ ___ ___

BUILD − B + S + O − I − D = ___ ___ ___ ___

BAAL + L − B − A = ___ ___ ___

HOUSE − H + Y − S + R − E = ___ ___ ___ ___

MOUNT − O + I − T + D − U = ___ ___ ___ ___

WHEN + D − WH + A − E = ___ ___ ___

CARMEL − C − RM + L − E = ___ ___ ___

BURNED − ED − B + Y + O − N = ___ ___ ___ ___

STRETCHES − TC + N + G + T − ES = ___ ___ ___ ___ ___ ___

MARK 12:30 _____

_____

A Very Special Guest

2 KINGS 4:17-37

> YOU are a little boy whose best friend is Azzur. (A-zhur)
>
> He is the son of the Shunammite woman who is a friend of the prophet Elisha.

The early morning sun touches the top of the mountain, pouring its light, like golden honey, down the sides of the mountain and into the valley below.

"Isn't Mount Gilboa beautiful this morning?" YOU ask YOUR best friend Azzur.

He nods in agreement. "I'm so glad that we can see it right from our house here in Shunem."

You are both sitting on the flat roof of Azzur's home where you have spent the night sleeping under the bright stars. As YOU roll up YOUR sleeping mat, YOU peek into the upper chamber, built on the rooftop.

"Has Elisha been here as your guest lately, Azzur?"

"No. My mother says she is hoping he will come again soon though." Azzur stretches and looks toward the private room on the roof that his parents have made for the great prophet of God. "She says he always brings a special blessing when he comes."

"Like you, Azzur?" YOU tease, jumping just out of reach in case he wants to take a playful poke at YOU.

"Yes, like me—especially like me." Azzur laughs and shows off his muscles.

Azzur's name means "helper" and you both have made a joke of it, but YOU remember that it is because of his mother's hospitality to Elisha that God gave her Azzur as a blessing. YOUR thoughts are interrupted by a servant appearing at the top of the stairs.

"Young master, I thought you might still be here," he says. "Come, you must eat your breakfast. Your mother thought you would like to see

the reapers finish the harvest. She said you two can take lunch to your father in the field today."

Later that morning YOU and Azzur jog down the dirt road, raising little clouds of dust around you with every step. The sun is high overhead and the day is scorching. Azzur breaks into a run.

"Hurry! I can see the field and the reapers already," he calls back over his shoulder.

Sweat pours down YOUR face and stings YOUR eyes. YOU glance at YOUR friend in dismay.

"Slow down, Azzur. It's too hot to run," YOU complain.

Azzur must have really been in a hurry today, for YOU see he hasn't got anything on his head to keep off the burning rays of the sun.

His father welcomes you and generously offers to divide his lunch with both of you. YOU are just going to hint that YOU are hungry when Azzur suddenly begins to scream.

"My head! My head!" he cries in agony.

His father leaps to his feet in concern and calls to a servant, "Take my son home to his mother."

The servant nearly runs YOU down as he scoops up Azzur and sets off on the road back toward Shunem. YOU decide to go with the servant.

Azzur's face is flushed and he is saying all kinds of strange things. The trip seems to take forever. At last YOU race ahead of the servant and into Azzur's house, calling for his mother.

Time passes slowly. No one seems to be interested in eating now. YOU hunch, arms wrapped around YOUR knees, in a miserable ball of fear, staring at Azzur. His mother holds him on her lap as though he is a little boy again. She seems to have forgotten all about YOU as she cuddles him close, rocking back and forth. Azzur is quiet—too quiet. When YOU brushed against him on the way home, his skin was hot and dry and he was panting. Now his face is like carved ivory, as pale as the cool cloth on his forehead. YOU can't even hear him breathing. No! He just can't ... But then YOU watch his mother stand up and silently carry Azzur outside. YOU follow her up the stairs to the prophet's room and with tear-blurred eyes YOU see her lay him on the bed.

Events follow each other swiftly after that. YOU hardly realize YOU are tagging along with Azzur's mother as she and a servant rush to Mount Carmel to find Elisha. YOU are only thinking about YOUR friend back in Shunem.

Gehazi, Elisha's servant, comes running to meet YOU, but YOU brush past him, trailing Azzur's mother. Suddenly she dashes forward and throws herself at Elisha's feet. She begins to weep and talk about the prophet's promise and her son.

Elisha immediately sends Gehazi to Shunem with mysterious orders. "You must hurry and lay my walking stick on the boy's face. Don't stop to greet anyone along the way. Don't even answer anyone who greets you."

The prophet soon realizes that Azzur's mother will not leave without him, and so they speedily turn towards Shunem. Her servant walks behind them.

YOU join the sad little procession. YOU feel stunned and hollow. YOUR legs move numbly. YOU can only think of Azzur and see his pale, still face in YOUR mind again. YOU don't remember just how YOU get back to Shunem. What can the prophet mean by sending Gehazi to carry out such strange orders? What has Elisha got in mind? As if in answer to YOUR thoughts, YOU see the prophet's servant breathlessly running back to meet YOU.

Gehazi's face is filled with anguish. He gasps, "Master, nothing happened. The boy is still lifeless."

It seems like the end of YOUR world. Now YOU are forced to admit the awful truth. YOUR friend—YOUR best friend—is dead!

Elisha seems to ignore that fact. He determinedly continues to the house in Shunem. There he dashes up the outside steps to the room where he has spent so many happy hours as a guest.

YOU stand silently staring up after him. Azzur's mother goes into the house weeping. Gehazi stands, head bowed, under a sycamore tree in the courtyard. Should YOU go in the house? Or should YOU follow Elisha to see what he is doing? Then YOU decide—YOU sprint up the stairs two at a time.

The sun is so bright up here that YOU have to shade YOUR eyes. YOU see Elisha close the door behind him just as YOU reach the roof. YOU know YOU probably shouldn't do it, but YOU just can't help YOURSELF. Squinting, YOU peek in through the small window. YOUR eyes gradually adjust to the darkened room inside. What will happen next? What is Elisha going to do? What can possibly be done to help someone who is dead? THEN ...

Read 2 Kings 4:33-37 and write/tell the astonishing ending of this story as **You Are There.**

Fascinating Facts

An upper room such as the one built for Elisha in this story was a special place for distinguished guests. It was cooler in hot weather, quieter, and more private than the rest of the house. The Bible tells us that this guest house for Elisha had a bed, a table, a stool, and a lampstand.

Elisha seemed to enjoy visiting the home in Shunem much as Jesus did visiting with Mary, Martha, and Lazarus in Bethany.

When Elijah was taken to Heaven, Elisha asked God to give him a double portion of Elijah's spirit. God answered his prayer. Elijah did seven miracles, and Elisha did fourteen. No one else in Bible history did more miracles than Elisha, except Jesus himself.

Many years after Elisha had died and was buried, he raised another person to life. The story is told in 2 Kings 13:20-21. During an enemy invasion, a man was buried in the same tomb as Elisha. When his body touched Elisha's bones, the man was brought back to life!

Although the Bible doesn't specifically tell us what the boy died from, the symptoms described fit the problem of heatstroke. This illness affects people today in hot weather as it did in the time of this story.

Share and Compare

1. In the YOU story, who is YOUR best friend?_____

2. Read 2 Kings 4:17-36. Which of the following are YOU characters in the story and which are people actually mentioned in the Bible?
   Write their names in the correct columns.

   Azzur   Gehazi   Elisha   Father   Mother   the reapers

   YOU   BIBLE

   _____   _____
   _____   _____
   _____   _____
   _____   _____
   _____   _____

3. What does the name Azzur mean?_____ Why was the boy in the story given that name?_____

4. In the YOU story, what did Azzur forget to do?_____

5. Where did Azzur go to be with his father?_____

6. Circle the letter of each event that HAPPENED in the Bible story found in 2 Kings 4:17-36.

   a. Mother named the boy Azzur.
   b. Mother told the boy to take lunch to his father.
   c. The boy cried out in pain.
   d. The servant carried the boy to his mother.
   e. Mother took a donkey and a servant to find Elisha.
   f. Father asked Mother why she wanted to talk to the man of God.
   g. Gehazi laid Elisha's staff on the boy's face.

7. What does the Bible say was the matter with the boy?_____

8. Why do you think his mother laid Azzur on Elisha's bed?_____

9. In what special way did the mother approach Elisha?_____

10. Why do you think the mother would not leave Elisha?_____
_____

11. Read 2 Kings 4:29. Why do you think Elisha gave the servant, Gehazi, these special instructions?_____

12. Elisha ignored the fact that the boy was dead and continued to the guest room where he was lying. What does that tell us about Elisha and his relationship to God?_____

A-MAZING FAITH

In this Bible story, Elisha shows that he is a man with great faith in God. This maze game will help us learn more about faith.

See how many words you can find by following the lines between each letter. A letter may be used more than once. The letters may go forward, backward, up, down, or twist around. Two people may play. Keep lists of the words you find. The winner is the one with the most words.

Think about the words as you find them. Share how they help us better understand faith.

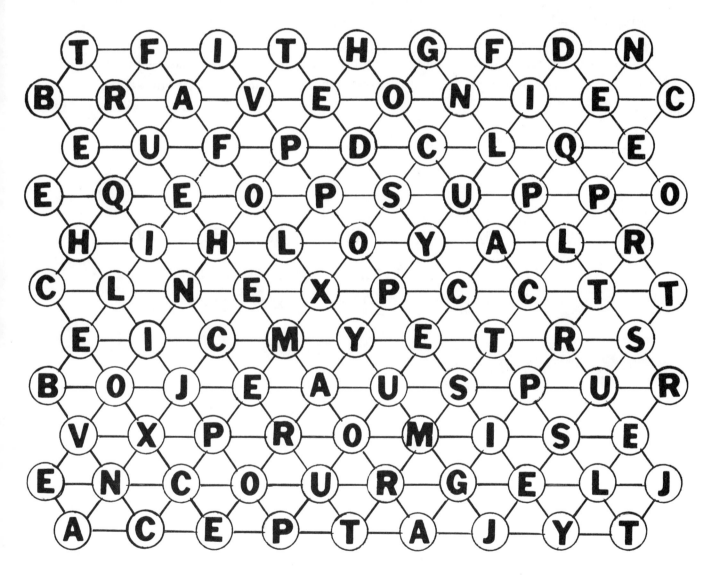

Here are some of the words in this maze:

promise	encourage	rejoice	support	rely
true	faith	accept	hope	pray
brave	cheer	Jesus	God	confidence
loyal	belief	expect	trust	help

Vanishing Vowels

Elisha prayed to God asking Him to bring the dead child back to life. He prayed, believing God would do what he asked, and, he acted on that belief. His whole life was based on faith. He did not wait to see proof that his prayers had been answered, but went ahead trusting the Lord for all his needs. That kind of faith was what inspired the child's mother to also place her trust in the Lord.

The apostle Paul was also a great man of faith. In the book of 2 Corinthians, chapter 5 and verse 7, he wrote about his own experience of believing God to supply his needs in all circumstances.

The verse is given for you below, but the vowels have all vanished. See if you can write the verse by supplying the correct vowels for each word in the spaces provided.

"W_ L_V_ B_ WH_T W_ B_L__V_,
N_T B_ WH_T W_ C_N S_ _."
2 C_R_NTH_ _NS 5:7

Now cover up the verse and try it again, this time filling in the consonants instead of the vowels. No peeking allowed. I believe you can do it without looking back at the other verse!

"_E _I_E _Y __A_ _E _E_IE_E,
_O_ _Y __A_ _E _A_ _EE."
2 _O_I_ _ _IA_ _ 5:7

A Servant Who Shared

2 KINGS 5:1-15

YOU are a boy who is a slave to Naaman, the captain of Syria's army.

YOUR good friend is Abiah (a-BY-uh), the little Israelite slave girl to Naaman's wife, Shua (SHOO-uh).

YOU check once again just to be sure everything is prepared. It is, and YOU say, "All is ready for our journey, Master."

Naaman turns to say goodbye to Shua, his wife. YOU see Abiah standing near her mistress. What is she thinking about today?

YOU remember the first time YOU saw this little girl, Abiah. Captain Naaman and the Syrian Army had just returned victorious from a raid upon Israel. They had brought back many captives from that land to be used as slaves. And Abiah had stood there, head held high, with a look of hope on her face. While the other captives slumped dejectedly in silent despair, or wailed bitterly, she had a look of great peace. Perhaps that difference in attitude is what made Naaman choose her as a personal servant for his wife.

Whatever the reason, YOU are glad that Abiah became one of the household servants. Although YOU are older than she, you soon became good friends.

"Don't you ever feel sad, and lonely for your home, Abiah?"

"Oh, I miss my family and friends very much, but God has put me here and given me a kind mistress. He is with me here—not only in the land of Israel. Sometimes, though, I feel very sad when Master Naaman returns from worshiping in your temple of Rimmon."

"Sad? Why should you be sad, Abiah? Shouldn't we worship the great god of thunder and rain who causes plants to grow and gives us food to enjoy?"

"I am sad because you do not know the one, true God—Jehovah. Master Naaman needs to know about Him because then he would not have to be what he is—a leper."

"How can you say such a thing! Do you think that your god is stronger than 'the Thunderer'? Do you dare say he can heal our master's terrible skin disease?"

"Oh yes. I know He can. Why, His prophet can even cause iron to float and poisoned food to be turned to good food again. He ... "

"Enough!" YOU shout angrily. "You are just an ignorant slave—and a girl at that." YOU point YOUR finger accusingly at her. "You had better keep to what you are here for—waiting upon Mistress Shua. How dare you claim such a thing for your god? Is he not the same god who let you be captured and taken as a slave by the great Naaman? I don't want to hear any more about your god or his prophet."

YOU thought that settled the matter. Abiah had just looked at YOU and said nothing, but YOU saw her brush a tear from her cheek. Was she just crying because YOU hurt her feelings? Or could she really care about a man who was her enemy and would die if no cure were found for his awful disease?

Then one day as Abiah served Mistress Shua, she told her about the prophet of God. "If only my Lord Naaman were to go to the prophet in Samaria, I know he would be healed!"

Well, that did it! Mistress Shua told Master Naaman, and he told the King of Syria. The king then wrote a letter about Naaman to the King of Israel. Before YOU had time to think about it, YOU were put to work with some of the other men servants to prepare for today's journey.

When YOU finally had a chance to talk to Abiah alone, YOU were really upset. "Do you realize what you've done? Because of your silly, wishful thinking, the two most important men in Syria think your god can heal an incurable disease."

"But it isn't just a wish. I know the prophet of God can do this. Didn't I tell YOU how he brought a young boy in Shunem back to life?"

"Perhaps. I just don't know what to think. Do you realize what will happen if this mission fails? Do you? Well, what do you have to say now?"

Her eyes were clear and trusting as they met YOUR troubled stare. "But it won't fail." YOU started to stomp off when she added, "I'll pray."

Now YOU pick up the reins of the team of horses and help Naaman into the chariot beside you. As YOU lift the whip and start off, YOU get a final look at Abiah's upturned face. It is filled with peace.

The trip from Damascus to Samaria is long, but at last you wait outside the palace of Jehoram, King of Israel. As YOU care for the horses, YOU overhear some of the guards discussing the letter from the King of Syria.

"The whole thing is ridiculous. A king isn't a god who can heal people of incurable diseases. They say only Jehovah can do that."

"Well, even if a king could do such a thing, Jehoram isn't the right man for the job. His palace is full of ivory carvings of Egyptian gods and goddesses, but I daresay he isn't on speaking terms with any of them—much less having Jehovah hear him. I do wager, though, that he would do almost anything to get his hands on those gifts of silver, gold, and festal garments the Syrians brought for the one who cures this Naaman."

"I say it's just a trick by Syria to start a war. What is the king doing about these trouble-makers?"

"The rumor is that the prophet Elisha has asked them to be sent on to him. He says they will soon know there is a prophet of God in Israel."

It proves to be more than a rumor, and soon you are waiting outside the prophet's door. What great thing will he do to cure Naaman? Maybe he will wave his rod over him, chanting a magical prayer. He might even command fire from heaven. YOU wait in great excitement to see what happens next.

At last the door opens and out steps a servant. "My master Elisha says you are to go and wash seven times in the Jordan River and you shall be healed."

Naaman is furious. "What kind of prophet is this? I have come all this way with gifts and a royal request, and I do not even get a glimpse of the man! If I have to wash in a river, I will wash in our own rivers in Damascus. At least they are clean." He jumps into the chariot and snatches up the horses' reins.

YOU know that Naaman is a proud man and this command of the prophet's is very humbling for him. Then YOU remember Abiah's faith in God and this prophet.

YOU take a deep breath. With sweaty palms and lowered eyes YOU approach Naaman. "My father, if the prophet had told you to do some great thing, would you not have done it? How much more then, when he tells you, 'Wash and be cleansed.'"

YOU have taken YOUR life in YOUR hands. What will Naaman do next? THEN . . .

Read 2 Kings 5:14-17 and write/tell the miraculous ending to this story as **You Are There.**

Fascinating Facts

Leprosy is a skin disease that causes ugly sores. Before the days of modern medicine, it could prove fatal to those who had it. Naaman's leprosy must not have been very catching, because he was not isolated because of it.

Even though Naaman had this terrible disease, the King of Syria still chose to walk with him to worship his god, Rimmon, rather than walk with anyone else. This shows us just how much he valued Naaman's friendship.

When Naaman was told to go bathe in the Jordan River, he said that the Abana and Pharpar rivers of Damascus were better than all the waters in Israel. The Abana is a river with many waterfalls coming from the mountains northwest of Damascus. It and the Pharpar, with their cool, clear waters, are the sources of the beauty and lush vegetation of Damascus. Arabic writers often refer to this area as "the garden of Allah." (god)

On the other hand, the Jordan River is muddy and dirty. If Naaman only needed to bathe seven times in water to heal his leprosy, you can understand why he wanted to return to Damascus rather than bathe in the Jordan.

Share and Compare

1. Read 2 Kings 5:1-15. On the line below write the names of the people NOT mentioned in the Bible.

   Shua   Abiah   Naaman
   King of Syria   Elisha   King of Israel

   _____

2. What disease did Naaman have?_____

3. Where did Naaman live?_____

4. Read 2 Kings 5:2. How did the little girl become a slave?

   _____

5. Why do you think the slave girl told her mistress about the prophet of God?

   _____

6. In the YOU story, Abiah had some definite reasons why she believed the prophet of God could cure Naaman's skin disease. Can you name some of those reasons?_____

   _____

7. Read 2 Kings 5:6. Whom did the King of Syria tell to heal Naaman?_____

   _____

8. What was Naaman told to do in order to be healed?_____

   _____

9. Why do you think Naaman was so unwilling to do what Elisha commanded?

   _____

10. Read 2 Kings 5:13. What reason did the servants give Naaman for trying what he had been commanded to do?_____

    _____

11. Read Galatians 5:22-23. What fruit, or fruits, of the Spirit do you think the little slave girl in this story showed to her owners?_____

    _____

12. What do you think we can learn about God from this example of the little slave girl?_____
    Is this a good thing to know?_____ Explain._____

    _____

Witness Watchers

Jesus said that people will know we belong to Him if we have love for one another. In each situation below, there is an opportunity to show love. How would you show that love in each case? Remember, people are WATCHING to see if you love Jesus by the way you treat others!

Your little brother has been bothered by a bully at school. Every day at lunch, this boy forces your brother to give him his dessert. How can your little brother show love in this bad situation?

_____

_____

Jodi just started taking drugs. She says it helps her forget her parents' divorce and gives her a good feeling. Nicole is concerned about Jodi and wants to help her stop taking these drugs. Jodi will listen to Nicole because they are best friends. What should Nicole do to show love and concern for Jodi?

_____

_____

Your youth group wants to have a service project to help the homeless and needy people in your area. You are in charge of drawing up a plan to meet the needs of these people and actively involve your group. What are some things you would list in this plan?

_____

_____

When we are Christians, other people watch us to see if we demonstrate the love of Jesus in our daily living. What are some ways you show love to others? List some of them here. If you find your "love life" needs improvement, ask God to show you ways to be loving towards others in your actions each day.

_____

_____

Witness Wrap-Around

The little Israelite girl was a caring witness in Naaman's household. Even though she was a slave far away from her homeland, she continued to love and worship the Lord. She looked for ways to share His great love with others.

As you make this wrap-around memory verse, imagine that God is wrapping His arms around you in love.

DIRECTIONS:

Using the pattern, cut a sturdy piece of cardboard (such as the back of a writing tablet) for the verse. Cut notches on your cardboard where shown. Print the words of the verse on it just like the pattern. Punch a hole at the top where the small circle is and tie one end of a 55 inch piece of string in it. Following the verse order, wrap the string from one notch to another. To make this wrap-around self-checking, draw the lines on the back of the cardboard as shown on that pattern. You said the verse correctly if the string covers the lines on the back of your wrap-around.

"God loves you. So always do these things: Show mercy to others; be kind, humble, gentle, and patient." Colossians 3:12

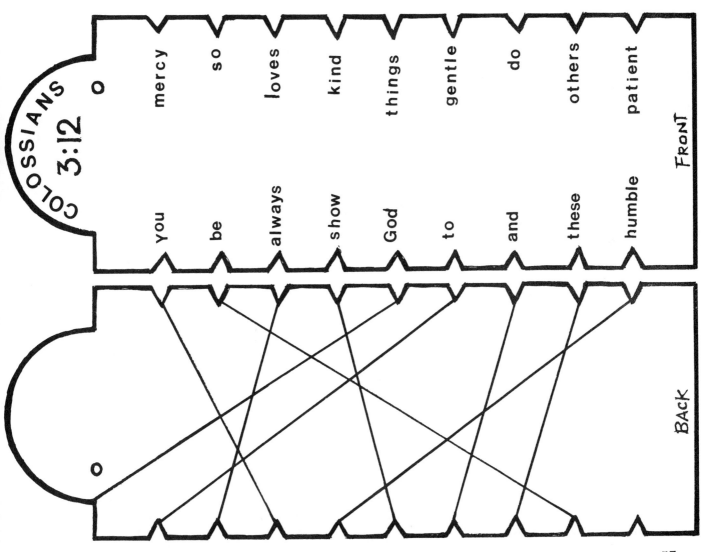

Go Lay a Brick

NEHEMIAH 2:12-20; 4:1-23

YOU are Eri. (AIR-ee)

He is an Israelite boy living in Jerusalem. His family is one of many who returned to live there after being captives in Babylon.

YOU creep silently along the trail that winds through the city's ruins. It's late at night, but in the moonlight YOU can see a man riding a donkey just a little ways in front of YOU. He is too busy looking at the broken stone walls to pay attention to YOU. The few men with him don't see YOU either. It's a good thing they don't, because YOU are supposed to be home asleep.

Well, YOU did go to bed, but it was too hot in the house to sleep. YOU were just taking YOUR mat up to the cool, flat, rooftop when YOU saw this man and his companions go by. YOU recognized them as the strangers who came to Jerusalem three days ago.

Tonight YOU followed them out of the city through the Valley Gate, by the Dragon Well and Trash Gate, toward the Fountain Gate, and to the King's Pool. Now they have stopped for some reason. YOU shrink back into the shadows and listen to what they say.

"It is even worse than what you told me, Hanani. There are broken walls everywhere."

"Yes, Nehemiah, every gate so far has been burned beyond use."

"Why here it is so narrow between the debris, there isn't even enough room for the donkey to get through. We must turn and go up the valley. Then we'll go back and re-enter by the Valley Gate again."

YOU watch them turn away. YOU have seen enough. It would be best to slip back into the city and be on YOUR sleeping mat before YOU are missed. At least YOU don't have to worry about a guard at the gate. No one has bothered to guard Jerusalem's gates for a long time. It would be useless. The walls are so broken down,

enemies can enter the city anywhere they desire.

Later, as YOU finally settle down to sleep, YOU can't help but think about what YOU have seen tonight. Who is this Nehemiah? Why is he inspecting the walls? And why at night? What is he really up to? Perhaps tomorrow YOU can find out what this is all about.

The next morning YOU get answers to YOUR questions, because Nehemiah has summoned everyone in Jerusalem to a meeting.

"My fellow Jews, we are in serious trouble. Our city is little more than a ruin. The walls are mere jagged stone teeth that can't keep our enemies out. The gates are only fit for firewood."

People around you sadly nod in agreement. YOUR father sighs. "It is indeed a terrible shame."

But Nehemiah has more on his mind that criticizing Jerusalem. "I am the personal cupbearer to his majesty, King Artaxerxes, and he has sent me here from Persia to help you. We can rebuild the walls. Then we won't be ashamed anymore."

YOU stare at YOUR father in amazement. "If he's just a servant, how can he help us rebuild the walls?"

"Shh, Eri, I want to hear all that he has to say."

. . . .

It is now evening and YOU and YOUR family are eating. "Nehemiah said the king gave him permission to get timber from the royal forest to build the wall and its gates. Are we really going to rebuild them, Father?"

"Yes, Eri. It's almost too good to be true. It will certainly make Sanballat, the Samaritan, angry. He doesn't want us Jews to rebuild Jerusalem. He hates us for returning and taking over land and cities the Samaritans have claimed for themselves during our captivity in Persia.

"But are we going to start rebuilding now? It's almost harvest time."

"Nehemiah thinks if we work together we can

be done by harvest season," says YOUR mother. "And remember, even the women will help with the work."

"But what can women or children do? The blocks are much too big for them to move."

She just smiles. "YOU will see. There are many other things to do."

The very next day, the work begins. Every family is assigned to work on the part of the wall nearest them. Priests, Levites, goldsmiths, perfumers, sons of district rulers, merchants—everyone works together. First of all, the old ruins must be cleared away. Women give drinks of water and help pile up smaller pieces of trash for the men and animals to haul away. YOU are busy running errands and handing tools to the workers.

In the quarry nearby, huge limestone blocks are cut and smoothed for the wall. The soft limestone cuts easily and becomes hard with exposure to the air. YOU can hardly believe YOUR eyes when YOU see that each brick fits perfectly against the other without even needing mortar to hold them together.

But while the Jews are busy working, their enemies are busy plotting ways to stop them. Tobiah, the Jewish-Ammonite Governor, and Geshem, the Arabian ruler, join forces with Sanballat.

At first they make fun of the new walls. "Ha, even a fox could break down that stone wall. It's nothing but trash and ashes."

Then they use threats of attack. Nehemiah leaps into action. "One-half of you people will build. The other half will stand guard. We will place a soldier with a trumpet close by to warn of danger. Don't be afraid. The Lord is great and He will help us."

YOUR father becomes very tired. "I am going to lie down for a little while, Eri. I've been working with one hand and carrying my sword in the other."

"Father, aren't you going to at least put your weapon away?"

"Not now. We must stay alert."

At last the enemies give up their attack plan. They try to trick Nehemiah into an ambush. However, he isn't fooled. When Sanballat threatens to tell the king that Nehemiah is trying to become the king of Israel, Nehemiah is courageous.

"He will not believe you, Sanballat. He knows and trusts me."

They even bribe the priest, Shemaiah, to try to deceive Nehemiah into thinking they will kill him and that he should hide from them in the temple. That would shame him as a coward.

Nehemiah remains unafraid. "I won't do it."

YOU are really impressed by Nehemiah. "He is a wonderful leader isn't he, Father? He isn't afraid of anything."

"That is because he has such faith in God, Eri. He makes us believe we can do the work with God's help, and so we do it."

But will the wall be finished before the harvest? What will your enemies try next? Can Nehemiah really win? It seems impossible. THEN . . .

Read Nehemiah 6:15-16 and write/tell the courageous ending to this story as **You Are There.**

Fascinating Facts

Nehemiah held a very important position in the service of King Artaxerxes of Persia. There were often assassination attempts upon the kings of the ancient world by their enemies. In these endeavors, poison added to the king's food or wine was a frequent means of death. As cupbearer, Nehemiah was personally responsible to see to it that the king's wine was not poisoned. Thus, King Artaxerxes' life literally depended upon Nehemiah's loyalty to him.

Nehemiah's reception, and the willing permission from the king for him to return and rebuild Jerusalem, may have been partly due to the influence of Queen Esther. She was the Jewish orphan girl who had become Persia's queen about forty years before this time, and was likely still alive. King Artaxerxes was her stepson. Her authority, and that of her cousin Mordecai, had given the Jews prestige in the Persian court. Perhaps the friendly and helpful attitude of this king could be traced back to her influence.

Share and Compare

1. Who are YOU following at the beginning of the story?_____

2. Why do you think Nehemiah inspected the broken walls at night? (see Nehemiah 2:10)_____

3. Write the number of the description in Column 2 by its match in Column 1.

   a. Tobiah_____   1. King of Persia
   b. Sanballat_____   2. Samaritan—enemy of Israelites
   c. Shemaiah_____   3. Companion of Nehemiah
   d. Artaxerxes_____   4. Arabian ruler
   e. Hanani_____   5. Cup-bearer to King of Persia
   f. Geshem_____   6. Priest—tried to deceive Nehemiah
   g. Nehemiah_____   7. Jewish-Ammonite governor

4. In the YOU story, why did the father say Sanballat hated the Jews?_____
   _____

5. Read Nehemiah 2:8. What did the king give Nehemiah to help build the walls?
   _____

6. Where did each family work on the wall? (see Nehemiah 3:10, 28-30)_____
   _____

7. In the YOU story, what work did the women do to help rebuild the walls?___
   _____
   What did YOU do to help in the rebuilding?_____

8. According to the YOU story, in what way were the stone bricks perfect?_____
   _____

9. Read Nehemiah 4:16-23. What orders did Nehemiah give the people when their enemies threatened to attack them?_____
   _____

10. What did Sanballat threaten to tell the king about Nehemiah?_____
    _____

11. How do you think Nehemiah could be so courageous no matter what his enemies tried to do to him and the Jews?_____
    Explain._____

12. How could you apply the truth learned in this lesson to a troubled situation in your own life? Give an example.
    _____

Courage Challenge

Every day we meet opportunities which challenge our courage in some way or another. Today you will have a chance to make vital decisions and face danger. Come along and discover how courageous you really are.

You are riding along a lonely country road on your bike in the late afternoon. Suddenly a small boy runs out in the road and calls for help. You can see he is very frightened. He explains that he and his friend, Tommy, were fishing by the river when Tommy slipped and fell into the water. Tommy has disappeared under the water and this boy, David, can't swim. Tommy needs to have help right away!

You are the only one available who can help Tommy. You can swim, but have never tried to save anyone before. Even if you find Tommy, he may need CPR. You have only seen people use that on TV. You can send David to town on your bike to bring help, but it is five miles to town and right at the time of rush hour traffic. You dash to the river bank with David and look around for anything that might be of help. What questions race through your mind? What choices will you need to make quickly? Now, use the rest of this page to help you meet this challenge.

1. Consider the problem carefully. What facts will help you decide what to do? List them here:

   _____

   _____

2. What is your plan of action? Can David be of some help? Use these lines to write out your choices.

   _____

   _____

3. Write an imaginary account of your rescue. You may want to include some of the following suggestions:
   How did you feel when you found Tommy?
   How did you get him back to shore?
   What problems did Tommy have when you got him on land?
   How did your quick thinking save his life?

   _____

   _____

   _____

   _____

Baffling Bricks

Nehemiah and the Israelites used huge, limestone blocks *(that we are calling bricks)* to rebuild the wall and buildings in Jerusalem.

Use the word-bricks at the bottom of this page to build a verse on courage.

Cut the bricks apart. Lay the correct brick on each numbered square to "build" the verse.

You may want to mount the bricks on heavy paper BEFORE you cut them apart to make them easier to work with.

Keep the building and bricks in a Zip-lock bag for simple storage.

```
              24

      21    22    23

16   17   18   19   20

11   12   13   14   15

6    7    8    9    10

1    2    3    4    5
```

```
              33

        YOU   HAVE

   TROUBLE.  IN   PEACE

     ME.  WILL  THE  THIS

WORLD!  HAVE  BRAVE!  YOU  WORLD  HAVE

CAN  BUT  DEFEATED  JOHN  I  IN  BE  16:
```

The Woman Who Dared to Be Different

ESTHER 7:1-8:2

> YOU are Reba. (REE-buh)
> She is one of seven special handmaidens to Queen Esther of Persia.

The smell of the roast lamb and fatted calf make YOUR mouth water. The table is heavily laden with gold and silver trays piled high with bread, figs, dates, pomegranates, grapes, and almonds. Other trays of melons add still more color to the banquet table.

"Have arrangements been made for the king's cup, Reba?"

YOU have been asked this question by Esther, the Queen of Persia. Although YOU are her slave, YOU are also her friend. "Yes, my lady," YOU answer. "His favorite gold one set with rubies and emeralds is ready. I have also placed a gold and ivory cup on the table for our special guest."

The queen's lovely face turns sad for a moment. Then she smiles at YOU. "That is good, Reba. Everything must be perfect for tonight's banquet with the king and Haman."

YOUR thoughts go back to a few days ago. Then, YOU would have given almost anything to enjoy a banquet such as this. YOUR stomach had rumbled and growled so loudly that YOU had looked around in embarrassment to see if anyone else had heard it. But YOU had laughed to YOURSELF when, right next to YOU, Hodesh's stomach had done the very same thing. After three days and nights of fasting, every one of the seven maidens who served Queen Esther had the same problem. But, for her sake, they had willingly gone without food or drink.

When she first became queen, you had all wondered what Esther would be like.

"Do YOU think she will be cruel, Reba?" Timna had asked.

"Oh, I hope she will not be vain like Queen Vashti, don't you?" Hodesh had chimed in.

"We will just have to wait and see," YOU had answered.

Esther soon proved she was not at all like Vashti. Instead of taking pleasure in her power and authority over you, she seemed to be rather surprised that everyone would obey her slightest command. She was always polite and kind in her conversation, even to the lowest slaves. It was not long before she had won the hearts of her maidens by her love and genuine concern for them. It was a pleasure to do her will.

Then there were the wonderful stories she told to pass away the many long hours of the day. Everyone hurried to carry out each day's duties so that she might have time to hear a special story from Queen Esther about the God who created the world and heard the voices of His people in prayer.

Then came the day when the king's gate-keeper, Mordecai, was not at his post of duty. If there was one thing you could always count on, it was that Mordecai was at the gate. YOU saw him pass the queen's rooms every day on his way to work. Somehow, Esther always managed to be at her window when Mordecai passed by. YOU noticed that he never neglected to look up and salute her. They seemed to have a special relationship. But now, Mordecai was missing.

"He was found outside the king's gate, crying and wailing bitterly, my lady, YOU reported. "He was dressed in sackcloth and had put ashes over his head."

Esther was very upset. "Quickly, Reba. See that new robes are sent for Mordecai. Something must be very wrong for him to act this way."

But Mordecai had refused to wear the robes. Instead, he sent Esther a message by Hatach, the king's servant, who attended the queen. The message was a strange one indeed.

"The Jewish people are all to be destroyed. Haman, the king's best friend and next in command, has promised to pay a huge amount of money into the royal treasury to see that it is done. The king has given Haman his ring as a promise that it will be just as Haman wishes.

Mordecai urges you, Queen Esther, to go to the king and plead with him to save the Jews. He even called them your people," Hatach informed her.

Esther's face grew pale. "But I can not do that. You must tell Mordecai that the king has not sent for me for thirty days. If I go to him on my own, I can be killed. No one can approach the king and live unless he has called for him. No one except ... "

"Except whom, Mistress Esther?" YOU interrupted anxiously.

"Except the one to whom he holds out his golden scepter, Reba."

The queen's servants all feared for Esther's life after that. Mordecai's reply brought an alarming warning.

"'You are a Jew and cannot keep silent. You cannot escape even if you are in the king's house. God will deliver His people somehow if you refuse, but you and your father's house will die. And besides, who knows but that you have been placed in the kingdom for just such a time as this?' Those were his very words, my queen," Hatach declared solemnly.

Esther stood silently for a moment. Then she made her choice. "Tell Mordecai that he is to command the Jews to fast for three days and nights, and that they must pray to Jehovah for me. I will go in to see the king. If I die, I die." Then she turned to YOU. "Reba, will YOU and the other maidens also join me and fast?"

YOU answered quickly, "Yes, my lady, I will. I know they will also."

Esther prayed to Jehovah all through those long days. YOU found yourself also praying to Him. When King Xerxes held out his golden scepter to her as she approached him, YOU chose to worship and obey her God as YOUR God.

Her request to the king was simple and surprising. "My lord, will you and Haman come to a banquet in your honor?"

The king had been delighted to accept her invitation. That banquet was held last night. Now, tonight, a second banquet has been prepared for the king and Haman. YOU wonder what Esther has in mind. What is her plan? Will she plead for her people, the Jews? Will

her God—YOUR God—hear her prayers and save her life and the lives of all the Jews?

YOUR thoughts are interrupted as the king and Haman are announced at the door and escorted to the banquet table. YOU hurry to attend Queen Esther.

"Reba, will you please pour the wine?"

"Gladly, my queen."

Nervously, YOU pour the wine into the three royal cups. YOUR hands are shaking so badly YOU almost spill the wine on Haman. YOU pray silently to God, "Save Queen Esther. Please, Jehovah, hear her ... MY ... our prayers." THEN ...

Read Esther 7:1-8:2 and write/tell the exciting surprise ending to this story as **You Are There.**

Fascinating Facts

The name Esther means "star."

It has been estimated that there were about three million Jews in the Persian Empire at this time. The total population of the empire was about one hundred million.

The capital city of Shushan was also where Daniel had his vision and Nehemiah lived as an exile.

King Xerxes punished the rebellion of Babylon by destroying the Temple of Marduk which stood near the Tower of Babylon and is mentioned in the story of Daniel. This temple, with its golden idol of Bel and golden table, had helped to give the city of Babylon the nickname "City of Gold."

Historians and archaeologists have found that the details of the palace and court life found in the book of Esther are true to actual Persian customs. Even the titles of the government officials are correct. Ancient Persia is the country of Iran today.

Jewish people today still celebrate the victory of Esther and Mordecai over their enemies with a holiday called the Feast of Purim.

Share and Compare

1. In the YOU story, who are YOU?_____

2. Who is Esther?_____

3. The following people are mentioned in the YOU story. Put the number of the description in Column 2 by its match in Column 1.

    a. Vashti_____   1. King of Persia
    b. Mordecai_____   2. Previous Queen
    c. Hatach_____   3. Slave who attended Queen Esther
    d. Haman_____   4. God of Jews
    e. Xerxes_____   5. King's best friend
    f. Jehovah_____   6. Gatekeeper at palace

4. Why did Mordecai mourn and put on sackcloth and ashes?_____
   _____

5. What did Mordecai want Esther to do?_____
   _____

6. Why do you think the seven maidens who served Queen Esther were willing to go without food or drink for three days and three nights as she did?_____

7. Read Esther 7:2. What did the king offer Esther?_____
   _____

8. What did Esther ask the king to do for her? (see Esther 7:3)
   _____

9. Read Esther 7:1-8:2. Put the following events in the proper time sequence by writing the letter of the statement in the correct numbered blank.
    a. The king hangs Haman.   1. _____
    b. Esther invites the king and Haman to two banquets. 2. _____
    c. Haman begs Queen Esther to save his life.   3. _____
    d. King Xerxes gives Mordecai his own royal ring.   4. _____
    e. The king takes a walk in the palace garden.   5. _____
    f. Esther sets Mordecai over the household of Haman.   6. _____

10. A gallows is a wooden frame with a rope noose, used for hanging criminals. Whom did Haman intend to hang on the gallows he built?_____

11. Why do you think Esther dared to tell the king she was a Jew, when the Jews were all condemned to die?_____
    _____

12. What does the surprising end of this story tell us about God?
    _____

Faithfulness Filmstrip

Queen Esther was faithful to God even when it might have cost her her life. She influenced other people around her because she prayed and acted in faith. She depended on God to help her.

Choose one of the problems below and create a filmstrip to show how you could remain faithful to God in that hard situation.

1. You are offered drugs. "Be like everyone else. Try it just once!"
2. You are with a friend who dares you to steal an item from a store. "The store has insurance for it anyway. They won't lose any money."
3. You are asked to play a trick on a refugee child in your grade. He doesn't speak English. "He's too dumb to know the difference."

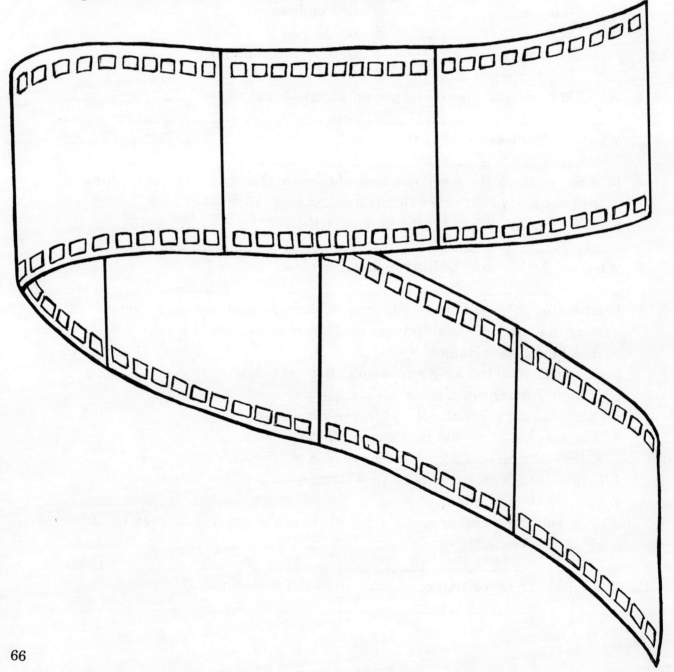

Loyalty Lineup

Another word for faithfulness is loyalty. Queen Esther was loyal to the Lord and spoke out for Him even when her life was in great danger. God does not forget the people who love Him.

The following word lines are printed in a special way. See if you can line them up correctly and rewrite them, as they should be, in the blanks above the letters.

Then memorize the verse as a promise from God. Claim it when you face tests of your loyalty to the Lord.

"THE LORD SAYS,

'IF SOMEONE LOVES ME,

I WILL SAVE HIM.

I WILL PROTECT

THOSE WHO KNOW ME.'"

PSALM 91:14

The Ten-Day Vegetable Diet Plan

DANIEL 1:5-20

> YOU are Eliel. (EL-ee-el)
> He is one of the Hebrew boys taken as captive by King Nebuchadnezzar of Babylon. Along with his friends, Daniel, Mishael, Azariah, and Hananiah he is receiving special training at the king's palace.

"Are you coming, Eliel? We are supposed to be in language class right away."

"I'm coming, Mishael." YOU take longer steps to catch up to YOUR two friends, Mishael and Daniel. YOU tell them, "I was just looking at the Ishtar Gate. It's really wonderful, isn't it? I'VE never seen such a huge gate in Judah."

"I suppose it is considered great, but anything built to honor an idol is of little interest to me," Daniel says.

"But, Daniel, you must admit those blue enameled tiles, with all the life-size dragons and bulls, are beautiful."

"Beautiful, yes, but of no more real value than the Temple of Marduk and its gold image of Bel. They are all man-made objects to worship false gods, Eliel. YOU, as a Jew, know there is only one true god—Jehovah. We must worship only Him!"

YOU glance around nervously. "Shh, Daniel. You'd better not let Ashpenaz hear you say that. He's been really kind in taking care of us here in King Nebuchadnezzar's court. But if he heard you talk like that, we would all be in trouble. This whole city of Babylon is full of temples and altars to gods and goddesses."

"That's true. But that doesn't mean we are to become like these people and worship their gods," chimes in Mishael.

"But—" YOU start to protest as you enter the palace classroom. YOUR friends just shake their heads and point to an empty space beside your other two close friends among the Jewish captives, Hananiah and Azariah. YOU hurry to sit down just as Ashpenaz, the king's chief officer, speaks.

"Today, each of you will receive a new name. This will help you adjust to your new life here. Each name will be taken from one of our gods so that you will receive his blessing during this three year training period. Azariah, you will become Abednego; Hananiah, you will be Shadrach; Mishael will become Meshach; Daniel will be Belteshazzar; and Eliel, you will be Tammuz."

Later that day, YOU and YOUR friends are waiting for the evening meal in your private room in the palace.

Hananiah shakes his head sadly. "New names acquired from false gods. What will be the next move to make us into good Babylonians?"

"It's not that bad," YOU say. "We can still call each other by our Jewish names when we're alone. I don't think it really makes that much difference."

Daniel disagrees. "Eliel, it makes a great deal of difference if we continue to allow them to reshape us into unbelievers like themselves. Don't YOU see? It is like turning our backs on Jehovah. I intend to remain Daniel, come what may."

Just then servants enter with food trays and set them down on the table. YOUR mouth waters as YOU look at the food. YOU are about to help YOURSELF to the delicious-looking beef sent from the king's own table, when Daniel grabs YOUR hand.

"Stop, Eliel. Don't YOU know what YOU are doing?"

YOU look puzzled. "No, I don't … Oh. Now I know what you mean. I forgot to ask Jehovah to bless the food."

Daniel is upset. "That's only part of what I mean. YOU'RE just about to eat food that's been offered to idols. We can't eat that. It's food Jehovah has expressly forbidden us to eat. Don't YOU understand? We must remain loyal to God, even here as prisoners in a heathen land."

"And just how do you intend to do that, Daniel? You're only 13 years old. Are you just going to march up to Ashpenaz and tell him the king's food doesn't measure up to your standards?"

"I might have to do that, Eliel. We have to draw the line somewhere. God will honor and bless us if we remain true to Him and His commandments. If we don't, then He will punish us."

"Ha!" YOU explode. "You're wrong. He gave us all of this to enjoy. But go ahead. Give it up. Be foolish. As for me," YOU say, reaching for the meat, "as long as I'm here in the palace, I intend to live like royalty."

Daniel looks at YOU sadly. He gets up and goes to the opposite side of the room where he kneels down and begins to pray. Hananiah, Mishael, and Azariah look from Daniel to YOU and back to Daniel. Then they go over by him, kneel down, and bow their heads.

The very next day Daniel is true to his word. He pleads with Ashpenaz, asking that he, Azariah, Mishael, and Hananiah be excused from eating the king's food. YOU know that they are all praying that God will help Daniel in this request. YOU just don't feel like praying to Jehovah these days. It is as if a wall has come between YOU and Him.

Ashpenaz is very troubled. "But I can't let you do that, Daniel. My master himself has ordered you to eat this food. If you don't eat it, you will become sick. You will be pale and weak compared to the other young men. And then, if the king finds out I have allowed you to do this, he will cut off my head!"

But Daniel persists. "Let us try eating only vegetables and drinking water for just ten days. And, at the end of that time if we aren't healthier than the other young men, then you will know how to feed us."

At last Ashpenaz agrees to a test period. "But only for ten days!"

YOU watch the four boys to see what will happen. It seems that the more YOU conform to life here in Babylon, the less YOU have in common with them. But, after all, shouldn't YOU do things the way the Babylonians do, when they are giving YOU every comfort possible, providing an expensive education, letting YOU live in the king's palace, and offering YOU an important government position?

YOU feel more and more out of place with Daniel, Azariah, Mishael, and Hananiah as the days go by. What will happen at the end of the test time? Will they get sick and cause the king to cut off Ashpenaz's head? Can Daniel be right that God will bless and honor those who obey Him? Will Jehovah punish YOU because YOU have turned YOUR back on Him? Ten days pass and THEN ...

Read Daniel 1:15-20 and write/tell the motivating ending to this story as **You Are There.**

Fascinating Facts

Daniel's Babylonian name, Belteshazzar, never really did stay with him. He had a position of authority in the governments of four kings during his lifetime: Nebuchadnezzar, Belshazzar, Darius, and Cyrus. In the Bible, all four kings refer to him as Daniel.

The capital city of Babylon was the most marvelous city of the ancient world. Its massive wall was sixty miles around and encompassed more than three thousand acres. The Euphrates River divided the city into two almost equal parts. The city was called "the City of Gold" because of the vast amount of gold used in its temples and images.

The great Tower of Babylon was seven stories high. When Nebuchadnezzar was king, this tower was already one thousand years old.

Nebuchadnezzar's queen was from a lush, green, mountainous country. She became very homesick in the flat Babylonian desert plain. In order to comfort her, the king had a series of terraces built that reached three hundred fifty feet in height. These terraces were covered with trees, flowers, and bushes that were irrigated by water being pumped from the Euphrates River to a reservoir on the top terrace. There were beautiful fountains, and even artificial rain was produced by a sprinkling system. These "hanging gardens" were built during the time Daniel was chief of the wise men of Babylon. They were one of the seven wonders of the ancient world.

Share and Compare

1. What is YOUR name in this YOU story?_____

2. Read Daniel 1:1-3, and 6. How did Daniel, Hananiah, Mishael, and Azariah come to be in the King's palace in Babylon?_____
_____

3. Daniel 1:4 gives a description of the main characters in this YOU story. On the line below, write some words that are used to describe them._____
_____

4. Write the number of the description in Column 2 by its match in Column 1.

    a. Daniel_____   1. King of Babylon
    b. Hananiah_____   2. Meshach
    c. Mishael_____   3. Belteshazzar
    d. Azariah_____   4. Shadrach
    e. Eliel_____   5. Chief palace officer
    f. Nebuchadnezzar_____   6. Tammuz
    g. Ashpenaz_____   7. Abednego

5. How long was the training period for the young men?_____

6. According to the YOU story, why wasn't Daniel impressed by the Gate of Ishtar, the Temple of Marduk, and the golden statue?
_____

7. Whom did the people in Babylon worship?_____

8. In the YOU story, the Tower of Babel is mentioned. Read Genesis 11:1-9. Why do you think God confused their language? (see verse 4)_____
_____

9. Why wouldn't Daniel eat the king's food? (see Daniel 1:8)
_____

10. Ashpenaz gave several reasons why he couldn't let the young men go on the special diet. Name some of those reasons._____
_____

11. What were the young men like at the end of the ten-day trial period?_____
_____

12. What can we learn from this story?_____
Would knowing this be helpful for life today?_____
Explain. _____

Dedication Diary

King Joash was another person who was dedicated to obeying the Lord. He repaired the temple and helped the people to worship Jehovah as they should. You can read about it in 2 Kings 12:1-12. Use the diary page to make brief entries that Joash might have written as the temple repairs progressed. References have been given to help you.

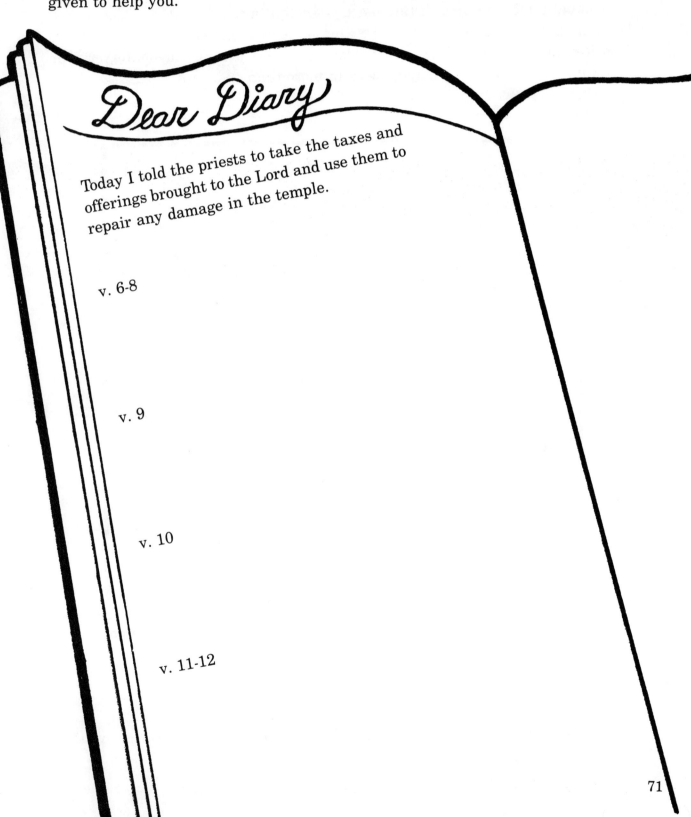

Dear Diary

Today I told the priests to take the taxes and offerings brought to the Lord and use them to repair any damage in the temple.

v. 6-8

v. 9

v. 10

v. 11-12

Dedication Deposit

Daniel was wholly dedicated to doing the Lord's will. His one desire was to be the person God wanted him to be. It didn't matter to Daniel where God put him. The Lord placed him in hard circumstances with heathen kings, but Daniel remained true to the Lord all his life.

If you put something in a certain place you might also say that you "deposit" it. The words to a Bible verse, about the kind of dedication Daniel had to God, are deposited in this puzzle. They are hidden up, down, across, diagonally, or even backward. The same letter may be used in more than one word.

```
L  L  E  W  J  P  B  D  L  O
T  Z  R  I  G  H  T  Y  G  M
T  B  S  L  N  E  H  T  F  Q
Y  H  U  L  P  W  G  O  V  N
D  F  I  S  Z  D  R  O  K  E
P  S  J  N  R  B  W  D  Q  H
U  D  O  O  G  Z  S  N  J  T
V  O  L  P  T  S  B  Y  L  R
J  M  Y  H  W  R  F  V  A  E
T  A  H  W  Z  D  N  A  Y  S
```

"Do what the Lord says is good and right. Then things will go well for you."
—Deuteronomy 6:18

Adventure at Sea

Jonah 1:1-17

YOU are the child of the captain of a ship which sails out of its home port of Joppa. Your father takes Jonah as a passenger on a voyage to Tarshish.

YOU blink and squint as YOU look out from the deck of the ship. The sun dazzles YOUR eyes as it reflects across the waves. It is a beautiful day for a sea adventure. Adventure! The very word brings visions of foreign cities, tastes of new foods, sounds of strange languages and music, smells of spices and flowers, and the touch of sea breezes. YOU may see dolphins at play. There are sure to be steep coasts and dangerous rocks. There might even be pirates. YOU think back about that special day that started this adventure.

"How would YOU like to go along with me when I sail to Tarshish?" YOUR father had asked. "I think it's time for YOU to see what a cargo ship is like."

YOU didn't even have to think it over. YOU wanted to go!

YOU had felt very grown-up as YOU packed an extra change of clothing and told YOUR friends goodbye. YOU could see they were all wishing they could go along.

Now, YOU are in the busy city of Joppa. Ships from different cities are tied up along the shore. Slaves and laborers scurry back and forth, like a line of busy ants, as they carry wine, wheat, olive oil, balsam, honey, and figs aboard your ship and store them carefully in the cargo hold below the deck. Sea gulls squabble among themselves as they snatch dropped bits from the loads.

YOUR father gives the long-awaited order to the sailors, "Cast off."

YOU feel a thrill of excitement as the ropes are loosened and the ship glides away from the shore. YOU think for a moment about the strange man who is the only passenger with

you on this trip. He was so defiant and yet frightened as he paid YOUR father his ticket money. He kept glancing behind and around him. Then he fled down the rope ladder to the cargo hold in the lowest part of the ship. YOU surely wouldn't want to be down there. Why that must be the hottest, most uncomfortable, uninteresting place of all!

The trip is indeed wonderful. YOU soon get used to the roll of the ship and enjoy the tangy sea breeze that leaves the taste of salt on your lips. YOU wonder if the eyes painted on each side of the ship's bow can really help it see where it is going.

As the day goes on, however, the weather quickly changes. Now thick black clouds mask the sun. Thunder growls in the distance. Occasionally a flash of lightning rips the greenish sky. The sails crack and the mast groans in return. It reminds YOU of a cruel taskmaster's whip across the back of a struggling slave. The wind becomes a screaming monster. This is not at all the delightful voyage you expected.

"Hold on tight, youngster," an old sailor calls to YOU. "YOU could be washed overboard."

The sailors are alarmed and begin to cry out prayers to their gods for help. YOU are terrified. To which gods should YOU pray? There are many from which to choose.

Then the rain comes down in torrents. The storm is fully upon you now.

YOU can scarcely hear YOUR father above the howling wind as he shouts to the sailors, "Throw the cargo overboard." He turns to YOU. "Come with me below deck."

The cargo hold is a mess. Barrels are rolling back and forth. The neat stacks of supplies are buckling and toppling everywhere. YOUR father discovers the passenger, his cloak wrapped around him, curled up sound asleep on the floor in one corner of the hold.

He swoops down, seizes the man, and shakes him. "What is this? How can you still be asleep? Get up and pray to your god so all of us will not be killed."

Later a sailor reports, "The cargo is all thrown overboard, sir."

Still the wind grasps at the ship and shrieks from every direction. It looks as if the ship is going to be torn into pieces.

"You, passenger, up on deck," your father orders.

YOU scurry up the ladder after YOUR father and the man. The sailors gather around the three of you. It is decided to cast lots to find out who is responsible for this dreadful storm. This reveals the passenger as the guilty man.

He hangs his head in shame. "I confess I am indeed guilty. I am a Hebrew named Jonah, and I fear the Lord, the God of heaven, who has made the sea and the dry land. I am running away from Him because He told me to go to Nineveh and tell them how wicked they are. I know it is my fault that this storm has come. God has chased and caught me."

"Nineveh!" YOUR father bellows. "But that's in the opposite direction. It is many miles from the sea. Why, you cannot even get there by taking a boat. They have their own god—Dagon. I hear he is half man and half fish."

"Dagon?" YOU ask. "Isn't he the god who is also named Oannes or Ioannes? Why that is almost the same as your name—Jonah. How very strange."

"All right, Jonah," YOUR father demands. "Tell us what to do to you to quiet this storm."

Jonah slumps in despair. "You must throw me into the sea and God will stop the wind."

YOU can't help but feel sorry for the disobedient man. So does YOUR father. Instead of doing what Jonah says, he orders the sailors to try to row the boat to shore. But the harder the crew rows, the worse the wind swoops down upon the ship like a gull after a fish. At last, YOUR father orders the sailors to stop rowing. He gathers them once more around the rebellious, horror-stricken Hebrew.

Lifting his face toward the angry, black sky, YOUR father shouts above the roaring wind. "Oh, Lord, God of Jonah, we pray we may not die because of what we must do to this man. We do it in obedience, not in anger. Have mercy upon us!"

YOU wonder what kind of a god this man Jonah must worship. If he is truly the god who made the sea and dry land, how could anyone ever run away from him? Will he hear YOUR father's prayer? Can he really stop this frightful storm? If so, he must be a wonderful god indeed. And what will become of this man, Jonah? YOU can hardly believe what happens next because THEN . . .

Read Jonah 1:15-17 and write/tell the unusual ending of this story as **You Are There.**

Fascinating Facts

Nineveh and its surrounding suburbs may have had a population of up to six hundred thousand people. This is approximately the size of the city of San Francisco, California, which has six hundred seventy-eight thousand people. Water for the city was brought from mountains thirty miles away.

Rumor was that a wall over one hundred feet high and over sixty miles long surrounded the city. This wall was so wide that three chariots could ride side by side on its top.

The palace of Nineveh had seventy-one rooms.

The word sometimes translated as "whale" in this Bible story is better translated "great fish."

An actual account of a whale swallowing a sailor was reported in 1891 by a ship named *The Star of the East.* James Bartley, the sailor, fell into the sea while whaling. He was found alive in the whale's belly three days later when the crew cut the sperm whale up for its blubber.

Share and Compare

1. Why are YOU excited in the beginning of this story?_____
   _____

2. What kinds of things does the boat carry on its voyage?_____
   _____

3. Read Jonah 1:1-13. Which of the following people are actually mentioned in the Bible? Write their names on the line below.

   ship captain   slaves   laborers   Dagon   Jonah   sailors
   _____

4. Why do you think Jonah didn't want to go to Nineveh?_____
   _____

5. Where was the ship going?_____ Why is that important?
   _____

6. Why do you think Jonah hurried down into the bottom of the ship?_____
   _____

7. Who sent the great wind? (see Jonah 1:4)_____

8. Read Jonah 1:13. Who showed more concern for other people than Jonah did for the people of Nineveh?_____

9. Write the letters of the events that happened in BOTH the YOU story and the Bible, on the line below.

    a. The trip started out on a bright, sunny day.
    b. Slaves loaded the boat with cargo.
    c. The boat sailed from Joppa.
    d. A great wind threatened to destroy the boat.
    e. The sailors prayed to their gods.
    f. The cargo was thrown into the sea.
    g. Jonah was asleep during the storm.
    h. The sailors tried to row the boat to shore.
    i. Jonah was afraid of the storm.
    j. The ship captain prayed to Jonah's God for mercy.

   _____

10. What happened when Jonah was thrown into the sea? (see Jonah 1:15-17)___
    _____

11. Read Jonah 1:16. The sailors stopped praying to their gods and worshiped the Lord. What made them change their minds about which one was the true God?
    _____

12. What can we learn from this story of Jonah?_____

JOURNEY OF OBEDIENCE

"If you love me, you will do the things I command." —John 14:15

Apologized to Mom. Ahead 3

Pulled tail of friend's cat. Back 1

Collected papers for teacher. Ahead 1

Took friend's pencil. Back 1

Picked up baby's toys. Ahead 2

Lied to parents. Back 3

Shared snack with friend. Ahead 2

START

JOPPA

Gossiped about classmate. Back 2

Took out trash. Ahead 1

Tripped little sister. Back 2

Talked to new classmate. Ahead 3

Sassed Dad. Back 3

NINEVEH FINISH

We show our love to God when we are obedient to His words. These words center on caring for others. Two or more may play this game. They will need a die and markers. Throw the die and move the number of spaces shown. If you land on a space with directions, you must obey them. The player to FINISH first is the winner.

76

Mirror Message

In this YOU story, the ship's captain was surprised that Jonah had taken a boat to Tarshish when God had told him to go to Nineveh. Nineveh was in the opposite direction and could be reached by traveling on land. This was direct disobedience on the part of Jonah.

When we look in a mirror, we see things just the opposite of the way they really are. The memory verse below is written in mirror writing. Rewrite each word correctly and you will discover a promise for you from God. This promise can be claimed by obeying God in whatever He asks you to do.

OLD TESTAMENT ANSWERS

Note:

Answers are not given to questions where the students are to think for themselves. You will notice that the numbers do not run in sequence in those instances.

Mission Impossible
1. Keren-Happuch
2. Rebekah
3. 12
4. moon god
5. the Lord
6. husband
7. 2, 5, 6, 7, 3, 1, 8, 4,
9. betrothal

Trust Tangle — "Depend on the Lord. Trust him, and he will take care of you." — Psalm 37:5

Mystery of the Silver Cup
1. Joseph, Grand Vizier of Egypt
2. return their money in the grain sacks
3. Joseph stored grain before famine
4. Benjamin
5. Joseph's brother
6. seated in order of age
7. hide it in Benjamin's sack
8. g, c, b, d, a, f, e
9. used by some to explain dreams and tell future
10. become Joseph's slave

Mummy Mystery — "If someone does wrong to you, then forgive him. Forgive each other because the Lord forgave you." — Colossians 3:13

Follow the Red Sea Road
1. man of the family
2. didn't make enough bricks with straw
3. Egyptians, mountains, sea
6. blood, frogs, lice, flies, sick and died, boils, hailstones, locusts, darkness, killed
7. terrified
9. behind Israel, before Egypt
10. east wind divided sea

Wandering Words — "Be like those who have faith and patience. They will receive what God has promised." — Hebrews 6:12

Once More, With Feeling
1. Joshua
2. gateway to west
3. great walls
6. Mother, Asher, Father, Merab
7. 6
9. march around Jericho 7 times, blow trumpets, shout
10. Lord gave them the city

Obedience Originals — Peter, Samuel, Abraham, Esther, Noah, Saul (Paul), Moses, Gideon, Rahab

Obedience Orbit — "I am waiting for you to save me, Lord. I will obey your commands." — Psalm 119:166

Just One More Chance
1. Irijah
2. Samson
3. 4, 1, 2, 6, 3, 5
4. harvest festival
5. his long hair
6. he lost his strength when his head was shaved
7. make him grind grain
9. 3,000
10. his hair grew back, God gave him back his strength Reverse Rewrite — "You must change your hearts and lives! Come back to God and he will forgive your sins." — Acts 3:19

Follow That Arrow
1. ceremonial ram horn, announce Feast of New Moon
2. Hesed — Prince Jonathan's slave
3. 4, 3, 5, 1, 2
4. sing and play for him
5. kill him with a spear
6. he was giving up the position as future king
7. d, a, c, f, b, e
8. tell the boy the arrows were beyond him
9. hidden in a field
10. so David couldn't become king

Active Arrows — "Our love should not be only words and talk. We should show that love by what we do." — 1 John 3:18

The Contest
1. The Lord, Jehovah
2. YOUR cousin
3. about who is God — Baal, or Jehovah?
4. burned new-born babies as sacrifices, sacrificed babies and built their bodies into their walls, cut themselves with swords and spears, danced, played wild music
5. Baal worship had to be stopped because of such cruelties
6. b, d, g, c, f, a, e
7. Mount Carmel
8. thinking, busy, traveling, sleeping
9. 12, same number as the tribes of Israel
11. prove that Jehovah was the God of Israel, prove Elijah was his servant, show people He had told Elijah to do all this, answer Elijah's prayer

Christian Connections
Across — (1) Blackwell; (4) Elliot; (7) Geronimo; (8) Luther; (9) Bunyan; (10) Key; (11) Lousma; (12) Sanders; (13) Whitman
Down — (2) Liddell; (3) Chase; (5) Tyndale; (6) Moody; (7) Grant; (9) Booth; (10) King

Counting Commitment — "Love the Lord your God with all your heart, all your soul, all your mind, and all your strength." — Mark 12:30

A Very Special Guest
1. Azzur
2. Pretend—Azzur
   Bible—Gehazi, Elisha, Father, Mother, the reapers
3. helper, mother helped Elisha
4. cover his head
5. the field
6. c, d, e, f, g
7. it doesn't say
9. caught hold of Elisha's feet

Vanishing Vowels—"We live by what we believe, not by what we can see."—2 Corinthians 5:7

A Servant Who Shared
1. Shua, Abiah
2. leprosy, harmful skin disease
3. Syria
4. taken as a captive
6. prophet caused iron to float, turned poisoned food to good, brought boy back to life
7. King of Israel
8. wash in the Jordan River 7 times
10. would have done a great thing, so why not this?

Go Lay a Brick
1. Nehemiah and Hanani
3. 7, 2, 6, 1, 3, 4, 5
4. hated Jews for returning and reclaiming land from Samaritans
5. a letter to get timber from the king's forest
6. next to them
7. gave drinks, piled trash, ran errands, handed tools to workers
8. needed no mortar to hold them together
9. carry tool in one hand and weapon in other, sleep in Jerusalem, gather when trumpet blown

Baffling Bricks—"You can have peace in Me. In this world you will have trouble. But be brave! I have defeated the world!"—John 16:33

The Woman Who Dared to Be Different
1. Reba—Esther's servant
2. Queen of Persia
3. 2, 6, 3, 5, 1, 4
4. Jews were to be killed
5. ask king to save Jews
7. half his kingdom
8. come to a banquet
9. b, e, c, a, d, f
10. Mordecai

Loyalty Lineup—"The Lord says, 'If someone loves me, I will save him. I will protect those who know me.'"—Psalm 91:14

The Ten-Day Vegetable Diet Plan
1. Eliel
2. captured and brought there for training
3. from important family, from king's family, healthy, young, Israelite, physically perfect, handsome, well educated
4. 3, 4, 2, 7, 6, 1, 5
5. 3 years
6. were man-made articles to worship false gods
7. all kinds of false gods and goddesses
9. make him unclean—not pleasing to God
10. get sick, become weak and pale, king kill him for letting them try it
11. very healthy

Adventure at Sea
1. YOU are going on a voyage with YOUR father to Tarshish
2. wine, wheat, olive oil, balsam, honey, figs
3. ship captain, Jonah, sailors
5. Tarshish, opposite direction of Nineveh
7. The Lord
8. the sailors
9. c, d, e, f, g, h, j
10. Jonah was swallowed by a big fish
11. the sea became calm

Mirror Message—"Go everywhere in the world. Tell the Good News to everyone."—Mark 16:15